Taking Charge of Your Career

Women *at* Work

Inspiring conversations, advancing together

The **HBR WOMEN AT WORK SERIES** spotlights the real challenges and opportunities women experience throughout their careers. With interviews from the popular podcast of the same name and related articles, stories, and research, these books provide inspiration and advice for taking on topics at work like inequity, advancement, and building community. Featuring detailed discussion guides, this series will help you spark important conversations about where we're at and how to move forward.

Books in the series include:

Making Real Connections

Male-Dominated Workplace

Next-Level Negotiating

Speak Up, Speak Out

Taking Charge of Your Career

You, the Leader

Women *at* Work

Inspiring conversations, advancing together

Taking Charge of Your Career

Harvard Business Review Press
Boston, Massachusetts

Printed in the United States of America

10 9 8 7 6 5 4 3 2

Library of Congress Cataloging-in-Publication Data

Names: Harvard Business Review Press, issuing body.
Title: Taking charge of your career.
Other titles: Taking charge of your career (Harvard Business Review Press) | HBR women at work series.
Description: Boston, Massachusetts : Harvard Business Review Press, [2023] | Series: HBR women at work series | Includes index. |
Identifiers: LCCN 2022028341 (print) | LCCN 2022028342 (ebook) | ISBN 9781647824648 (paperback) | ISBN 9781647824655 (epub)
Subjects: LCSH: Career development. | Women employees. | Success in business. | Occupations.
Classification: LCC HF5549.5.C35 T33 2023 (print) | LCC HF5549.5.C35 (ebook) | DDC 650.14—dc23/eng/20220812
LC record available at https://lccn.loc.gov/2022028341
LC ebook record available at https://lccn.loc.gov/2022028342

ISBN: 978-1-64782-464-8
eISBN: 978-1-64782-465-5

The paper used in this publication meets the requirements of the American National Standard for Permanence of Paper for Publications and Documents in Libraries and Archives Z39.48-1992.

CONTENTS

Introduction

Charting Your Path xi

A fulfilling career starts with you.

by Amy Bernstein, cohost of *Women at Work*

SECTION ONE

Make Your Own Way

1. **How to Build a Career You Won't Hate** 3
   Successful careers don't happen by accident.
   by Michelle Gibbings

2. **Four Questions to Help Women Navigate the Second Half of Their Careers** 19
   Questions to help anyone rethink and achieve their professional goals.
   by Palena Neale

3. **Finding a Job When You Don't Know What You Want to Do Next** 27
   A framework to provide structure and intentionality.
   by Mimi Aboubaker

4. **Going Out on Your Own** 39
Hard-won lessons to learn from.
A conversation with Stacey Abrams and Lara Hodgson

SECTION TWO
Be Your Own Career Coach

5. **What to Do When You Don't Feel Valued at Work** 49
It's okay to use the word I.
by Rebecca Knight

6. **Early Career Advice We Could All Benefit From** 57
Learn to balance assertiveness and persuasion.
A conversation with Paige Cohen

7. **How to Ask for the Job Title You Deserve** 65
Your compensation package—salary, perks, responsibilities, and title—is an ongoing negotiation.
by Rebecca Knight

8. **Get Comfortable Playing Office Politics** 73
Shifting your mindset can be empowering instead of icky.
by Lisa Zigarmi, Julie Diamond, and Lesli Mones

9. **Are You Taking On Too Many Non-Promotable Tasks?** 87
Don't miss out on the work that actually grows paychecks and careers.
by Linda Babcock, Brenda Peyser, Lise Vesterlund, and Laurie R. Weingart

10. **When Being Indispensable Backfires** 95
Make yourself present for the career moments that matter.
by Mita Mallick

SECTION THREE

Build Your Support Team

11. **Start Building Meaningful Connections** 103
The five relationships you need to invest in.
by Jenny Fernandez and Luis Velasquez

12. **How to Find a Mentor** 113
Mentorship can be life-changing.
by Janet T. Phan

13. **Build Chemistry with Your Mentor** 123
It will help the relationship reach its full potential.
by Janice Omadeke

14. **Network with People Outside Your Industry** 131
New connections will create more "career insurance."
by Dorie Clark

SECTION FOUR

Embrace Change and Uncertainty

15. **Take Time Off Between Jobs** 139
Downtime will reset the course of your career for the better.
by Rebecca Zucker

16. **When You Need Time Off for Health Reasons** 149
Focus your conversation on how your illness affects your job—and your plan for addressing it.
A conversation with Laurie Edwards

17. **Returning to the Workforce After Being a Caregiver** 157
Make it clear that this break was time out—*not time* off.
by Rebecca Zucker

18. **A Detour Doesn't Have to Compromise Your Goals** 165
Four strategies to regain control of your career arc.
by Dorie Clark

19. **When a Major Life Change Upends Your Sense of Self** 171
Embrace your new identity, and move forward with confidence.
by Madeline Toubiana, Trish Ruebottom, and Luciana Turchick Hakak

20. **Learn to Get Better at Transitions** 181
Plan for all the (inevitable) changes.
by Avivah Wittenberg-Cox

Notes 189
Index 193
Discussion Guide 207
About the Contributors 213
About the Podcast 223

INTRODUCTION

Charting Your Path

A fulfilling career starts with you.

by Amy Bernstein, cohost of *Women at Work*

For most of my career, I had no career plan. Sure, I wanted to be challenged and I wanted my work to matter somehow, but beyond that—nothing. I'd stick with a job as long as I was interested, and when I started to get a little too comfortable or a little bored, I'd take the next interesting job that came my way.

Then, when I was about to turn 50, I found myself in a role that just didn't feel right. The job didn't play to my strengths, and my work seemed to have little impact. I was busy but lost, with no sense of where I wanted to go. I was stressed out all the time and just plain unhappy.

How did I end up there? It was time for a reckoning.

I had to be honest with myself: I'd treated my professional path as an adventure without a destination and certainly without a map to get me there. This approach had to stop. In that moment, I decided to figure out what I wanted and to go for it. That's how I ended up in my current role at Harvard Business Publishing, where I believe in our mission, I'm proud of the work we do, and I like and respect my colleagues. Those are the priorities I identified for myself in that moment of feeling at sea, and so I set my sights on them. I finally took charge of my career, and am I ever glad.

If my story hits a little too close to home, then this book is for you. We put it together with early- to mid-career readers in mind, but the wisdom and insight you'll find in these pages will serve you at any career stage—particularly if you're seeking to understand your own ambitions and to find the best path to achieving your goals. This book isn't a road map or a step-by-step guide to charting your career path. Rather, it will help you understand the challenges you're facing and find ways through, over, or around them. No need to read this book from front to back; dip in and out as you feel the need for insight or inspiration.

Different sections of the book will guide you as you hit various crossroads. The first section, "Make Your Own Way," will help you face important professional and personal turning points—performance reviews, job changes, even milestone birthdays. I wish I had read chapter 2, "Four Questions to Help Women Navigate the Second Half of Their Career," as I was taking stock of my life in the weeks before I turned 50.

The four questions that author Palena Neale suggests we all ask ourselves would have done much to shape my soul searching: What would your career look like if nothing was in your way? What permissions do you need to give yourself to become who you want to be? How can you build and access your support network? And what do you need to learn? Had I had these questions to ponder, I'd have gotten where I needed to go much more directly.

Section 2, "Be Your Own Career Coach," is all about advocating for yourself—something women seem to have trouble doing. I spent the first 20 years of my career passively waiting for recognition, promotions, and raises to simply happen. Why did I think it was somehow unseemly to ask for what I wanted—what I *deserved*? I tended to be a good sport and made all the mistakes that the articles in this section warn against, like taking on the non-promotable tasks and never saying no to a request. As a wise mentor once told me, you don't get what you don't ask for. It took me way too long to see that he was right. You need to learn to advocate for yourself throughout your career. In fact, the earlier you start honing this skill, the more control you'll have over the way your path pans out. Check out this section if you're feeling underappreciated, underpaid, unpromoted, or generally undervalued in the workplace.

One important lesson I've learned is that you can't go at it alone—mentors, sponsors, competitors, and mentees are invaluable sources of support and inspiration.

Section 3, "Build Your Support Team," looks at the many connections you make or should make in your professional life. These relationships have sustained and propelled me, and as authors Jenny Fernandez and Luis Velasquez argue in chapter 11, "Start Building Meaningful Connections," they deserve your attention and investment. These relationships will grow with you as your career progresses. Strong connections can be the link to your next promotion or can support you when you take a career leap. Turn to this section of the book if you're trying to figure out how to build your network and foster the kind of mentoring relationships that will nurture you and help you take your career to the next level.

Even the most thoughtful and meticulous career planning is bound to get derailed by life, and that's particularly true for women. More than men, we deal with professional detours—to have and raise kids, to care for aging parents, and all those other pressing responsibilities that fall mainly to women. The last section of the book, "Embrace Change and Uncertainty," will help you deal with the turbulence that can blow you off course. Rebecca Zucker offers advice in chapter 17, "Returning to the Workforce After Being a Caregiver," for example. And Dorie Clark helps you see how a detour—whether it's a job loss, an illness, or a relocation—doesn't have to compromise your goals. The chapters in this section will help you maintain your sense of self, even when you feel as if you've lost control of your career.

We also have to acknowledge that our complicated lives will repeatedly serve up what Avivah Wittenberg-Cox calls "moments of liminality"—turning points when we may find ourselves "struggling to let go of *what was* (identity, community, colleagues, and competencies) to embrace *what's next* (as-yet unknown, undefined, and ambiguous)." We must learn to accept the "mixture of fear ('Who am I?') and excitement ('I am *so* ready for a change'), confusion ('What do I want?') and certainty ('Time to move on')." And we have to be astringently honest with ourselves and with those who support us about where we want to go, even as our goals will likely evolve. And we must take to heart this book's overarching message: Our careers will never give us the gratification and pride we want unless we decide to steer our careers ourselves. How I wish I'd known that all along.

SECTION ONE

Make Your Own Way

1

How to Build a Career You Won't Hate

by Michelle Gibbings

Every year, we start fresh with new hopes and dreams gleaming on the horizon—we're looking to get promoted, change jobs, or transition into a new role. How do we make our dreams a reality?

By developing a strategic, intentional, and flexible approach to our future. I call it a *career guide*: a well-thought-out plan highlighting what it will take to move our careers forward in ways that we find truly meaningful.

This approach has served me (and my clients) well throughout my time in the corporate world and now as an executive coach helping others make the leaps that will advance their careers.

Create Your Own Career Guide

Your guide will have four parts in total. Each part is meant to challenge you to think critically about what you want and where you should focus your energy. The ultimate goal is to identify your deeper purpose and skills and to take steps that will help you align your career with these.

Step 1: Write down your current career traps

In my work, I often come across people who are clearly trapped in their jobs. They know something's not working for them but struggle to pinpoint what that is or why it's so. I call these situations *career traps*, or patterns of thinking and behaving that we practice because they are familiar to us—even though they can hurt our productivity and effectiveness and lead to poor health and feelings of isolation. Chapter 10 describes how being indispensable at work can signal a career trap, and it suggests what you can do to fix it.

It often takes a crisis—a pandemic, getting fired, painful boredom, burnout, loss, or a significant illness—for us to stop, reflect, and recognize the career traps that might be tripping us up.

Burnout Isn't Just a Health Issue

A CONVERSATION WITH ART MARKMAN

When we think about what causes financial instability, we typically think about a business closing, a person losing their job, or an economic downturn. We don't typically think about burnout as a threat to our finances—but we should. Despite being on track to meet your retirement goals, if you burn out to the point where you can't do your job, you end up putting that financial safety net at risk. Goodbye, 401(k) contributions. Goodbye, rainy-day fund.

To learn how to prioritize protecting her retirement and savings from burnout, HBR editor Laura Amico spoke with Art Markman. He has written dozens of articles on topics including productivity, stress, and career management and is the author of Bring Your Brain to Work.

LAURA AMICO: Art, this idea, that burnout was a financial risk, now seems obvious, but it was new to me. Is this something you think about when you think about burnout? What is the real risk here?

ART MARKHAM: I think most people aren't really thinking about it. I think most people, when they think about the causes of financial instability, they're focused on, Will my business close? Will there be an

(continued)

economic downturn? Will Covid disrupt my industry in ways that might make it hard for me to make a living?

What they're not thinking about is, Will I reach a point where I get out of bed one day and say, "I can't go to work"? But that's a dangerous place to be, because when it happens, you're going to be drawing on savings and not continuing on the path to retirement that you thought you were on.

This really clarifies what I've been thinking about. For my entire career, I've thought my path to stability was going to come through work. But what I'm coming to grips with now is that my path to stability also includes not working so much.

As they used to say on the Saturday morning commercials, "It's part of a balanced breakfast." We need to find a balance between the energy we put into our work, and the energy we get back through other activities and through our interactions with family and friends.

For me, doing something every day that is decidedly not about work has been important. In April 2020, I was putting in 12-hour days, six days a week, at the University of Texas. I was part of a committee trying to figure out how the school was going to navigate the pandemic. At the end of each day, I went home and hopped on the absurdly expensive stationary bike I had bought when I realized the world was shutting down.

I sweated it out—whatever had happened during the day—for an hour.

I was trying to inject something that was not related to my job into every single day. It wasn't even the exercise per se. It doesn't have to be exercise. It can be anything that feels restorative. The less we do that is restorative, the lower our supply of resilience will be—and resilience can protect us from burning out.

What I hear you describing is a sort of resilience account that you need to build up by practicing restorative habits. Is that right?

I think that *is* right. On a daily basis, we have to try to make small deposits into that account. Many of us spend a lot of time thinking about how to use our vacation time. We assume that if we just make two big deposits—take two big restorative breaks—over the course of the year, then somehow we will be resilient enough to work the other 50 weeks without a real break. That's not realistic.

Of course, getting away from everything is great. A long weekend somewhere can be wonderful, but building your resilience and energy reserve is about the little things you practice daily. It's about taking an afternoon off when you need it to do something energizing and fun. Too often people work a half day, sign off, and spend the afternoon doing laundry or running errands. That's not effective in this

(continued)

context. If you're going to take a break, do something that's fulfilling.

I get that. But I have a 6-year-old and a 3-year-old. My PTO has gone to covering sick days and snow days—unplanned time off. Those days aren't especially restorative. Is there a way to make that time more fulfilling?

You can start by celebrating your accomplishments. Most people finish something and forget to pause and enjoy the feeling of achievement. We just move on to the next thing. This is true in the workplace, but it's true everywhere else too. When you finish making your bed in the morning or helping your kid with a homework assignment, for instance, take a step back. Take a snapshot of the moment, and let yourself think, "Wow. I checked this off my list, and I deserve to enjoy that feeling."

Another thing you can ask yourself is, "Are there fun ways to do what I need to do?" Can you play some music while you fold your clothes? Can you teach your kids a song you love and sing it together while you're cleaning the closet? Sometimes we trap ourselves by thinking, "Well, I just have to power through this. Let me get this done as quickly as possible." We distract our kids with a movie or an iPad, hoping they won't complain while we do whatever needs to get done. What if we let them participate? Your closet may not look as organized in the end, but you will have experienced some joy. There's a price to the efficiency we try to create.

Let me summarize a couple of the things that I've heard you say: Don't sweat the small stuff, celebrate your wins, and find ways to enjoy as much of it as you can—even the things that seem trivial. These are doable! Is there anything else I should be thinking about?

Just remember that everyone has a bad day sometimes. A bad day is not a sign of anything in particular, except that you're human. If the bad day turns into a bad week or a bad month, that's the point at which you should ask yourself whether you need a little more help managing your well-being. Reach out to a therapist or mental health professional if you need support. It's more than okay. It's a good thing.

That's great framing. When I reached out about this conversation, I thought we would be talking about taking time off, but your advice is more realistic. What you are advising is making daily deposits in my well-being account as well as my retirement account. And maybe the right mindset here is that frequent deposits in both accounts earn interest.

Yes. That's exactly right.

Adapted from "My Burnout Isn't Just a Health Issue. It's a Money Issue," on hbr.org, February 22, 2022.

Don't wait for a crisis to happen before you recognize your career traps. There are five common traps employees fall into. Be proactive by challenging yourself to consider whether these traps are impeding your progress.

- **Ambition trap:** You're a high performer who is used to success. You worry if you slow down, you'll stop achieving. Not knowing how to dial it back, you attempt a solution by working harder when the pressure at work rises.
- **Expectation trap:** You continually strive to meet other people's expectations. Consequently, admitting that you're struggling and overworked is ego-shattering. You worry that people will think less of you if you acknowledge you are burned out or unable to cope.
- **Busyness trap:** You enjoy being busy and consider it a part of your identity. For you, work always comes first. As a result, you struggle to say no, to slow down, or to switch off. You're likely to regularly sacrifice time with loved ones and your health for your job.
- **Translation trap:** You've worked hard to get to where you are, yet the happiness you thought you'd find eludes you. Despite all your hallmarks of success, you feel as if you have lost your way because your role doesn't fulfill or inspire you. Nor does it align with your purpose. At the same time,

you worry about changing directions because you believe that your current job is all you know.

- **Adrenaline trap:** You run your life on adrenaline, not taking enough time to care for your mind, body, and spirit. You are run-down and overworked. You say to yourself, "I'll take a break tomorrow," but tomorrow never comes. You have forgotten that putting your self-care needs first is a critical act of leadership and crucial for a sustainable career.

Avoiding these traps (and getting out of them) involves making deliberate trade-offs, and deciding on those trade-offs will become easier when you are clear on what matters to you. This brings me to step 2: figuring out your purpose.

Step 2: Define your purpose

Your purpose is your why—the reason you do what you do. For some of us, our purpose may be to lead a happy and healthy life. For others, it may be to create a life filled with learning and to pass on those lessons. Purpose can center around studying, experimenting, and trying new things. It can involve serving our communities, taking risks, or venturing into the unknown. Whatever our purpose, research shows that we can find meaning in our work by putting our why at the center of our decision-making.

So, what's *your* purpose? Answering this question isn't easy, and there's no magic formula. It is an iterative process that involves some soul-searching. To start, pay attention to what matters to you and motivates you. Ask yourself, "Why do I do what I do?"

When you answer this question, consider both your personal and your professional life. This holistic approach is essential because you can't divorce your work from the rest of your existence. A decision you make personally will affect you professionally (and vice versa).

If you feel the answer isn't apparent, dig deeper and ask yourself these other questions:

- What matters to me?
- What and who inspire me?
- When have I been the most motivated?
- What difference do I want to make through my work?
- When have I been most proud of who I am as a person?

Write down your responses, and look for themes or common threads. If you are more of a visual thinker, you might even try creating Pinterest boards for each question. The objective is to capture your thoughts, feelings, moods, and impressions. Your ideas don't need to be perfectly formed, as long as they have meaning. Over time, ideas will percolate, and the obvious answers will spill over. When that happens, you will know you have hit on something. It will feel right.

Once you know your purpose (which, by the way, can shift and change over time), you can be more intentional about dropping the habits that don't serve you (your career traps) and doing things that bring you closer to this purpose. When choosing a job or career path or saying yes to a new project, for example, you can ask yourself, "Does this align with what really matters to me? Does it get me one step closer to living a life aligned with my purpose?"

If the answer to those questions is yes, you know you are ready to move forward.

Step 3: Document your unique skills, and create your selling statement

Say you want to land a job that will stretch you and align with your purpose of *always learning.* To get that job, you will need to demonstrate to your prospective employer what makes you a good candidate and, more so, better than others who may be vying for that job.

Take some time to identify unique skills or your unique selling point—the things that, combined, make you better than your competition and would make any hiring manager pick you.

To find your own unique selling point, try this exercise:

- Divide a sheet of paper into two columns (or use Google Sheets or a Word file).

- In one column, list the skills and competencies you know you have. Include role-specific technical and functional skills (for example, programming, design, accounting) and non-role-specific competencies (for example, problem-solving, relationship building, creativity).
- For each item on your list, ask, "What value and benefit does this offer an employer?" and add your responses in the next column. For example, your digital skills may help an organization elevate its digital presence, or your strong relationship-building techniques may support a business looking to improve its customer engagement.
- Look at your experience and expertise, and highlight your greatest strengths—the specific skills that you do best and that make you an especially valuable candidate.

Once you have gathered all your data, use your analysis to start drafting what I call your *selling statement*, or a short explanation of who you are, what you stand for, and the value you can bring to any team, culture, or organization. Play with the words and sentences until you find a combination that accurately captures your essence.

Here are some short examples:

- I am an energetic sales professional committed to building strong and successful customer relationships. With a demonstrated record of identifying and nurturing potential leads and converting those into successful customer relationships, I create sustainable, high-quality revenue streams.

- I'm committed to making a difference by helping people learn and grow in their roles through my work. I'm skilled at creating a shared sense of purpose among my team members so we can deliver outcomes in a rapidly changing and complex operating environment. I do this by bringing the talents of each individual person to the forefront.

Your selling statement has multiple uses. You can use it as an elevator pitch for prospective employers and add it to your résumé or LinkedIn profile. Remember, though, crafting your statement isn't a one-and-done exercise. As you expand your skill sets and experience, you can and should revisit and rewrite your selling statement. Plus, what's valued by employers changes with time, so you want to ensure your unique selling point is current, meaningful, and targeted.

Step 4: Seize opportunities to expand yourself

Finally, make the most of every opportunity that comes your way. You don't need to say yes to every opportunity. But you need to be strategic and consider how the

Take Ownership of Your Learning

BY HELEN TUPPER AND SARAH ELLIS

Since we spend so much of our time, energy, and effort at our day jobs, they provide the most significant opportunities for learning. The challenge is that we don't invest intentionally in everyday development—we're so busy with tasks and getting the job done that there's no space left for anything else. Deprioritizing our development is a risky career strategy because it reduces our resilience, our ability to respond to the changes happening around us. Here are three ways to take ownership of your learning at work.

Learn from others

The people you spend time with are a significant source of knowledge. Creating a diverse learning community will offer you new perspectives and reduce the risk that you'll end up in an echo chamber. Set a goal of having one *curiosity coffee* each month, virtually or in person, with someone you haven't met before. The person could be someone in a different department and could help you view your organization through a new lens, or perhaps someone in your profession at another company could broaden your knowledge. You can extend your curiosity even further by ending each conversation with, "'Who else do you think it would be useful for me to connect with?" Not only does this question create the chance for new connections, but you might also benefit from a direct introduction.

Experiment

Experiments help you test, learn, and adapt along the way. There are endless ways you can experiment at work—for example, time-blocking when you read and respond to emails to minimize distractions, writing down a very small success at the end of every day to boost your belief, and increasing the speed of feedback with quick questions like, "When do you see me at my best?"

For an experiment to be effective, it needs to be a conscious choice and be labeled as an opportunity for learning. Keep a *learn-it-all log* where you track the experiments you're running and what you're learning along the way. Remember, you should expect some experiments to fail, as that's the nature of exploring the unknown.

Create a collective curriculum

In a squiggly career, everyone's a learner and everyone's a teacher. As a team, consider how you can create a collective curriculum where you're learning from and with each other. We've seen organizations effectively use *skills swaps*, where individuals share one skill they're happy to help other people learn. The swap could look like a creative problem-solver offering to share the processes and tools they find most helpful or lunch-and-learn sessions run by someone with expertise in coding. Skills swaps are a good example of democratized development where everyone has something to contribute and is learning continually.

Adapted from "Make Learning a Part of Your Daily Routine," on hbr.org, November 4, 2021 (product #H06OF5).

opportunity aligns with your purpose, goals, current skills, and the skills you need to build to get to where you want to go.

As part of this step, always be on the lookout for possibilities to expand your current role, and involve yourself in tasks you find stimulating. For example, you could volunteer to get involved in projects you are curious about or seek work that helps you acquire new skills. Take the initiative, and talk to your boss or other leaders to discover what's possible. As well as making your work more interesting, you'll be delivering more value than expected and, most importantly, broadening your network.

Successful careers don't happen by accident or without help from others. You need good people—and great people—around you to inspire, challenge, and support you along the way. Your network plays a crucial role in this support. Having a broad and deep network helps you expand your mindset about what's possible, more readily learn about how your industry and profession are changing, and identify where new opportunities are arising.

Now's the time to do the work. With your career guide drafted, your purpose at hand, and your attention focused, you will be ready to make this year your best year yet.

Adapted from "How to Build a Career You Won't Hate," Ascend, on hbr.org, February 8, 2022.

2

Four Questions to Help Women Navigate the Second Half of Their Careers

by Palena Neale

As an executive coach for a number of female leadership development programs, I work with purpose-driven women in every industry to identify their strengths and growth areas. While I've helped women of all ages, I've found that for many women in their fifties, the combination of newly empty nests, extensive professional experience, and financial freedom makes it the perfect time to finally accelerate their careers.

But that's often easier said than done. As a 50-something woman, what can you do today to reenergize your career and make the most of your remaining professional years?

What follows are four questions that can help anyone rethink and achieve their professional goals.

What would your career look like if nothing were in your way?

Your fifties are the time to invest in the second half of your life. Find a quiet, reflective moment to ask yourself some important questions:

- What's missing in your life? In your work?
- What kind of difference do you want to make?
- What does your dream job look like?
- What career move would you make if you knew you couldn't fail?
- What do you want to be remembered for?

Some of my clients dream about advancing into more-senior leadership positions, some envision creating a new, more fulfilling role for themselves, and others have considered leaving their organizations entirely to become entrepreneurs or focus on personal projects.

For example, Isabelle, a senior technical lead in a regional office, enjoyed an impressive career with several published books and key industry reference pieces.* At 52, she had just sent her son off to college, and she came to coaching for advice on how to make the most of her next 10 years. She recognized that she "had more time, energy, focus and freedom to reinvest in [her] work life," and she wanted to push herself out of her "narrow technical comfort zone" and focus on leading others.

With her son out of the house, she was no longer limited to local opportunities, so she started applying for jobs globally. In less than six months, Isabelle landed a leadership position in another country.

Another client, Florence, was a senior manager in a multinational organization. She came to coaching to talk about a troubling trend she'd been experiencing: Less competent, less experienced men kept moving past her into leadership positions for which she felt more than qualified. She was deeply committed to her organization and believed that by taking up a leadership position, she would be better poised to effect change both directly and indirectly by influencing others. She began actively promoting herself and applying for leadership positions in her organization, and after 14 months, she was asked to lead a major department.

What permissions do you need to give yourself to become who you want to be?

Many women get stuck in some version of the authenticity trap: They hold on to overly rigid definitions of a singular self, and these definitions don't permit them to engage with and develop other potential identities (for example, a leader) or skills (networking, managing, and so forth).

For example, Isabelle never allowed herself to ask for help, feeling that doing so would run counter to her core values of independence, autonomy, and strength. Florence prided herself in being someone who put her head down and got the work done, not someone who sought the spotlight. By questioning these limiting beliefs and exploring how they created unnecessary professional roadblocks, each woman was able to expand her identity and enrich her skill set.

Isabelle started to appreciate that asking for help signaled good leadership rather than a lack of independence. Instead of attempting to find a new job entirely on her own, she reached out to her boss, who turned out to be a supportive ally and introduced Isabelle to the hiring manager at her new organization.

Similarly, when Florence reframed her negative assumptions about self-promotion, she found approaches that aligned with both her goals of increased visibility in the company and her values of humility. After becoming more open to being in the spotlight, she enlisted her boss's support to present her team's work at a senior management retreat, joined a high-level working group, and presented her research at an international conference.

How can you build and access your support network?

At first, neither Isabelle nor Florence leveraged their networks to further their ambitions, so I urged both of them to conduct a relationship audit. The process is simple: Open a Word or Excel file (or grab a pen and paper), and write down as many names as you can for each category:

- **Career champions:** Who will sing my praises?
- **Sources of feedback:** Who will give me honest feedback on my performance and challenge me to develop?
- **Emotional support system:** Who will give me a positive boost?
- **Organizational sages:** Who will help me understand the ins and outs of the organization?
- **Mentors:** Who will help me think through personal and professional decisions?
- **Connectors:** Who has a large and diverse network and is willing to introduce me to others?
- **Power people:** Who has the power to make things happen?

After completing this audit, Florence reached out to colleagues who helped her identify new opportunities and connect with key decision-makers. Similarly, this exercise helped Isabelle leverage existing relationships to connect with important people both inside and outside her organization, ultimately leading to her new role.

The exercise was valuable not only because it helped both women identify useful contacts, but also because it allowed them to see how they themselves routinely supported others in their organizations. This new view enabled them to reframe networking as a shared, reciprocal activity rather than a purely transactional pursuit, making them feel more comfortable and confident with the process.

What do you need to learn?

Good leaders are constantly learning. What skills, information, or self-knowledge do you need to get to where you want to be?

For example, both Isabelle and Florence found that they had to upskill to meet their late-career goals. Updating CVs, preparing bios and LinkedIn profiles, and engaging on social media were all skills they needed to refine or learn from scratch. Not only did they gain valuable technical skills through this process, but the exercise also helped both women refamiliarize themselves with their professional accomplishments, building confidence and improving their ability to self-promote.

. . .

While I've focused on helping women who are looking to ramp up their careers in their fifties, this advice can apply to anyone. If you are a few decades into your career and looking to accelerate, think about what you want to be, do, and feel; recognize the beliefs and assumptions that might be standing in your way; and identify what new knowledge or skills will help you reach your goal. And when you compile an inventory of your supporters, don't forget to include yourself. You are your own strongest ally—so move forward boldly, and with no regrets.

**Names have been changed to protect privacy.*

Adapted from "4 Questions to Help Women Navigate the Second Half of Their Careers," on hbr.org, September 9, 2020 (product #H05UFF).

3

Finding a Job When You Don't Know What You Want to Do Next

by Mimi Aboubaker

Few people find embarking on a job search exciting. In fact, most of us would probably agree that it's a daunting and emotionally exhausting process. As a result, early-career job seekers tend to fall into two broad categories: avoiders and gatherers.

Overwhelmed by feelings of fear or confusion, avoiders often shut down entirely: "I don't know where to start, so I'm going to do nothing." Gatherers, on the other hand, respond to those same emotions with feverish action: "I have no idea what I want to do, so I'm casting a wide net," or, "I hate my current job, so I'll apply to everything."

Neither mindset is going to lead you to a successful outcome. In the case of avoiders, idleness does not result in job offers. For gatherers, a lack of clear direction leaves you wandering in many directions.

The Career and Personal Manifesto

To land a job you will actually enjoy doing, you need to be intentional about where you apply and why. As part of my own process, I've created what I call a *career and personal manifesto*, a framework to provide structure to any job search. You can use it, too.

The manifesto has three steps: (1) evaluate, (2) engage, and (3) execute. Let's take a look at these steps now.

Evaluate

A successful job search is simple. All you have to do is find job opportunities that match your needs and goals. The hard part is figuring out what those needs and goals are.

To start, spend time with yourself and evaluate potential next steps. Consider the following six categories, each of which include a series of questions to help you discover the factors most and least important to you in your next role.

As you answer these questions, think about your past and present jobs or internships and which aspects of each role you enjoyed most (or really disliked).

- **Environment:** What kinds of environments, management styles, and ways of working do you thrive in?
- **Role:** What kind of roles and prospects for growth are you looking for?

- **Compensation:** What's the minimum compensation you will accept, and what's your ideal range?
- **Skills acquisition:** What skills and competencies does your résumé currently demonstrate? Are you looking to gain additional skills or further specialize in what you know now?
- **Career narrative:** Where does your résumé position you in the hiring market? For example, does it suggest you're someone who cares about socially driven work? Does it suggest you're great at building, launching, and leading new initiatives? Have you collected "prestigious" company logos?
- **On the horizon:** Is there a meaningful and realistic step you can take within the next 18 months, in light of your answers? For example, are there opportunities you can take off the table or add?

Next, use your answers to these questions to fill out the *job search prioritization matrix* (see an example in figure 3-1). Completing the matrix will help you figure out which roles to prioritize as you move forward with your search.

Rank-order the six evaluation categories according to importance:

1. **Must-haves:** Required—will not consider any job *without* these items

FIGURE 3-1

Job search prioritization matrix

Use this tool to help you figure out what to prioritize in your next role. The example is for a junior consultant who is hypothetically interested in getting a job in the tech industry and who most values skills acquisition and the work environment.

Screening criteria

Reorganize categories according to importance of factor in your search

MOST IMPORTANT FACTORS ← → LEAST IMPORTANT FACTORS

HIGHER ↑	Skills acquisition	Environment	On the horizon	Career narrative	Role	Compensation
Must-haves Non-negotiables	**New skills:** Build creative problem-solving and critical-thinking capacities **Generalist:** Maintain generalist skill set	**Ways of working:** Dynamic environment; collaborative work streams **Feedback culture:** Continuous, informal feedback	**Entrepreneurship:** Want to build a company and looking to develop new skills critical to running a business	**Experience/skills:** Augment finance background with experience building and scaling a solution and team	**Experience:** Interviewing and hiring for different functions	**Total:** Maintain current compensation

Priority level

Organize attributes according to level of importance

LOWER

Nice-to-haves Added bonuses	**Opportunities:** Public speaking **Experience:** Launching new product or market for existing product	**Manager:** Direct; specific in providing instructions and direction **Team:** Disagreement is welcome and encouraged	**Team:** Develop deeper understanding of what it takes to be a highly effective startup employee **Team:** Learn how to coach and manage individuals with different skill sets	N/A	**Projects:** Expansion of service offering into new markets **Industry:** Transportation and logistics (freight, delivery, logistics)	**Equity:** Would be nice to have some ownership in next business
No-ways Avoid at all costs	**Responsibilities:** Financial modeling and presentation development (developed these skills previously in finance and looking to diversify skill set)	N/A	N/A	**Experience/ skills:** Deepening technical skills	**Projects:** Expansion of service offering into new markets **Industry:** Consumer products, consumer applications, personal finance companies	**Total:** Unable to take a step down in compensation because of family planning
Don't-cares Indifferent about these things	N/A	**Mission:** Not important in next role	N/A	N/A	N/A	N/A

2. **Nice-to-haves:** Important but won't make or break an opportunity

3. **No-ways:** Required—will not consider any job *with* these items

4. **Don't-cares:** Things that don't matter or are nonstarters

For instance, if compensation is the most important factor to you when you are searching for a new role, it should be the furthest to left on the matrix. Figure 3-1 presents an example of a matrix that has been filled out. This matrix is for a junior consultant who is hypothetically interested in getting a job in the tech industry and who most values skills acquisition and the work environment.

Engage

After working through the questions and filling out the matrix, you should have a better idea of what you are looking to do next. Now it's time to take action and start reaching out to people in your network. Discussions are a natural part of the job-hunting process, but you want to segment the people you engage with into two categories:

- **Thought partners:** People who can weigh in on your thinking and your path forward (mentors, alumni networks, former managers and colleagues, etc.)

- **Opportunity sourcers:** People who can help you identify open opportunities

When seeking outside counsel, be wary of what I call *advice of convenience*, or taking advice from people simply because they are in your orbit. Advice of convenience is an easy trap to fall into. Instead, try to step out of your comfort zone.

The best people to reach out to for advice are people who (1) you admire, (2) have demonstrated skills and personal attributes you would like to gain, or (3) are doing what you want (or think you want) to be doing. After all, who better to show you the path to where you want to go than the person already there?

Surprisingly, many people of all statures are accessible and enjoy offering career advice. There are a variety of channels you can use to reach professionals. The most tried-and-true is LinkedIn, where many professionals have an account. If you use this channel, include a personalized invitation to connect, explaining your objectives to increase the chances of a response.

The basic structure of your message should be as follows:

- Introduce yourself.
- Establish legitimacy by sharing context on your background.

- Clearly explain the purpose of your outreach, including why you want to connect with the recipient (for example, a specific job you have identified at their company, interest in their industry, or interest in learning more about their career path).
- Ask to meet either by phone or video call or in person.

Sticking with the preceding example of the junior consultant who is interested in transitioning into the tech industry, here is a LinkedIn message they might send to a hiring manager at a company they're interested in:

> *Hi Ben:*
>
> *I'm a second-year consultant with case work that includes working with education agencies. I'm looking to transition to EdTech startups, and Handshake piqued my interest.*
>
> *Would you be open to speaking with me sometime about roles that may match my skill set and interests?*
>
> *Appreciate any time you can provide and hope to hear from you soon.*

Industries such as technology, media, and fashion also heavily leverage social media platforms such as Twitter and Instagram. If the person you are interested in connecting with has a public account, you could send them a public tweet, comment on one of their posts, or send a private direct message, depending on your comfort level. A cold email—similar to the LinkedIn message above—is another option to consider. (Many years ago, I sent an Instagram direct message to the woman leading the U.K. fashion and luxury retail practice of a top technology company. I asked to meet her while I was in London. We did get together, and we're still in touch!)

People with whom you have some connection will result in higher response rates. These connections can be high school or college alumni or people with whom you share a tie through sports, a hometown or home state, culture, gender, Greek life, or a professional society.

Once a meeting time has been confirmed, be sure to send a calendar invite with all the appropriate details to the person you are connecting with. You want to make it as easy as possible for them.

Execute

At this stage, work with the contacts you have made in the preceding step to identify a few opportunities that are a good fit for you and the next stage of your career. Take another look at your evaluation criteria, and determine how your job prospects stack up against each other.

This is where the *opportunities prioritization matrix* comes in. Use it to organize the opportunities you find and prioritize those you want to apply to. This step will save you a great deal of time and energy in your search.

The opportunities prioritization matrix is a loose adaptation of the Eisenhower matrix. Here's how to set it up: Look back at the job prioritization matrix. Which two categories did you rate as most important to you? Place one of these categories across the horizontal axis, and the other along the vertical axis. Then decide if your opportunities rank high or low (meet or do not meet) those priorities.

The matrix has four quadrants of priority:

- **Focus here:** Opportunities in this quadrant are your dream jobs. Because they meet the two most important criteria you have identified, you should invest the most time pursuing these.

- **Waste of time:** Opportunities in this quadrant rank low for your most important criterion but may satisfy your second criterion. They may not even be worth applying to.

- **Be mindful of time invested:** These roles match your most important criterion but not the second. You will want to use discretion applying to these positions as well.

- **Distractions:** Naturally, you'll come across interesting opportunities that do not satisfy either of your two most important criteria. Try not to spend time applying to them.

If we use our original example of a junior consultant interested in moving into the tech industry, we know that this job candidate has an interest in mission-driven companies and has indicated in their job prioritization matrix that maintaining a generalist skill set and dynamic, collaborative environment are the two most important factors for their next job.

Figure 3-2 shows how the junior consultant might fill out the opportunities prioritization matrix if they were considering the roles shown for the various companies.

FIGURE 3-2

Opportunities prioritization matrix

Use this tool to help you prioritize which jobs to apply to. The figure below shows how a job candidate interested in mission-driven companies and maintaining a generalist skill set would prioritize various roles.

	High match skill acquisition	**Low match** skill acquisition
High match environment	**Focus here** **Handshake** Special projects **Guild Education** VP, chief of staff **Nova Credit** Enterprise sales	**Waste of time** **Handshake** Project manager **Guild Education** Product marketing **Nova Credit** Software engineer
Low match environment	**Be mindful of time invested** **GitHub** Strategy and operations **Stripe** Corporate strategy **PayPal** Chief of staff	**Distractions** **GitHub** Product marketing **Stripe** Senior financial analyst **PayPal** Software engineer

You can see that the job opportunities that offer generalist skills development (strategy, partnerships and sales, operations, etc.) and collaborative team environments land in the "focus here" quadrant. Job opportunities with a specialized skill set and less collaborative environment land in the "distractions" quadrant. Since social mission is also important to this candidate, mission-driven companies rank high on environment. Similar positions at non-mission-driven companies rank low when it comes to environment.

Of course, all companies and positions have tradeoffs. Structuring your matrix in this way allows you to stay laser-focused on only the two most important factors as you evaluate opportunities.

. . .

For even the most seasoned professionals, the multitude of career paths and job opportunities available can leave the job seeker immobilized. By using a structured framework such as this one to focus your efforts, you'll end up with a more favorable outcome and avoid becoming an avoider or a gatherer.

Adapted from "Finding a Job When You Don't Know What You Want to Do Next," Ascend, on hbr.org, January 28, 2022.

4

Going Out on Your Own

A conversation with Stacey Abrams and Lara Hodgson

Thinking about starting a small business? Or looking to expand a business you've already launched? Entrepreneurs Stacey Abrams and Lara Hodgson share hard-won lessons from starting and running three companies together. In this interview with *Women at Work* cohosts Amy Bernstein and Emily Caulfield, they reflect on what made their long-term partnership work well and how they manage self-doubt and guilt.

EMILY CAULFIELD: What do you think were the most important personal qualities that you brought to your entrepreneurship that made the difference in not only getting your businesses off the ground but then continuing to actually grow them?

LARA HODGSON: Without a doubt, I would say my two most important qualities are a curiosity for learning and a resilience/grit. And the second one, I didn't actually know I had until well into our series of starting businesses.

STACEY ABRAMS: I'd say for me, I am incredibly risk tolerant. I'm not a risk seeker, but I am very risk tolerant, which meant that when Lara had some just moonshot idea, that was always an important part of our relationship. I didn't start out in entrepreneurship. When we met, I was a lawyer. I was very happy with earning a paycheck, and so moving into entrepreneurship was a risk for me. And even though I'd started my own small company, going into business with someone, making it a permanent thing—rather than returning to a steady paycheck—was odd for me, but it was the risk-tolerance piece. One piece that always drew Lara and I together is curiosity: loving to learn new things, wanting to understand how things work and how to make them better, what a solution might look like, what new information might add to the equation.

AMY BERNSTEIN: Stacey, you said that your tolerance for risk and your shared zest for learning were important to the relationship that you and Lara have as you founded companies together. What is it that you would tell our listeners about how you make these partnerships work?

STACEY: We started out with rules, and those rules didn't come from long-standing friendships. A lot of partnerships begin with these long-term friendships, and you morph into a business partnership. Lara and I were friends: We knew each other, we liked each other, we could reach out to one another. But our friendship was built more on a mutual respect than it was on this longevity. But when we started working together, we had rules about how we would operate, what we would expect of each other.

One of the most important pieces of who we are is honesty. My caveat is that we do not have only honesty but transparency. Honesty is telling the truth. Transparency is telling the truth before you have to. We have a lot of transparency in our relationship where we don't wait for the hard question. We don't wait for the mistake to be uncovered. We get ahead of it. That has not only helped in our business relationship; it helps in our personal relationship with one another. But it also helps with our clients because we have this ethic that you don't try to hide from bad news, but you also have to be honest about the consequences and the catalyst.

Having a partner that you trust both emotionally and intellectually makes it much easier, and Lara's one of the smartest people I've ever known. Beyond just being a good businesswoman, I trust her intellectual integrity, and that also helped us work together because even when we disagree, which happens, we don't distrust the fundamental premise of the argument. We may disagree with the solution, but we don't doubt the other one's grasp of the challenge.

AMY: Lara, anything to add to that?

LARA: I would agree. A lot of people have a best friend that they've grown up with and their lives are aligned on all axes, and then they start a business together, and then they never have the space to step back from one another. With Stacey and I, we didn't necessarily go to the same church or have children in the same school. Our normal week allowed us time together, but it also allowed us time apart, and I think that's incredibly important because it preserves the diversity of our thinking. I think where a lot of partners go astray is they come together with diverse thinking, but then they spend so much time together that they actually lose their diversity. They lose that diversity of thought, and they start to think alike, and that's dangerous. Stacey and I always had the ability to approach a problem, appreciate the different perspectives, and then continue to develop those different perspectives by allowing our lives to have some distance.

EMILY: In your book *Level Up: Rise Above the Hidden Forces Holding Your Business Back*, you mentioned this idea of a sticky floor. You say that "sometimes what's holding you back is not a glass ceiling, but rather a sticky floor. Don't let your self-doubt overcome you." Can you talk about whether or not the two of you dealt with this in starting your businesses? And if you did, how did you deal with it?

LARA: I deal with it every day, and women and underrepresented founders tend to constantly question, "Am I good enough? Am I smart enough? Am I approaching it the right way?" And I think that's what is so valuable about our partnership because as individuals, you're always going to sort of wonder, "Am I missing something? Am I good enough?" So, I think our partnership both keeps us grounded when maybe we're worried about "Am I good enough?" But it's also there to keep you grounded when you're going off in left field and you need someone to say, "Bring it back in."

STACEY: One of the corollaries is that self-doubt is often driven by fear, and I believe in the legitimacy of fear. We are exhorted, especially for women in business, that you're supposed to be fearless. That is the dumbest advice. Because fears are real, and they are salient, and they come from something. One thing Lara and I do so effectively is we confront the fear. We don't ignore it. We don't pretend it doesn't exist, but we try to investigate the roots of it and figure out how we can befriend it. How do you navigate it? How do you leverage it? It's easier to do that when you have a business partner and a friend, but it's possible even if you're on your own. Both Lara and I came to this having done other projects independent of one another. And we brought with us both the fears that we had in those experiences but also the learnings from those fears and our willingness to share that with one another, but also what we learned the last time. Because part of the sticky floor is that you're fighting yourself, and you're fighting the legitimacy of those warnings. Fear exists because you're trying to tell yourself there's a danger. So, let's make sure you're not ignoring the warning signs. Instead, you're investigating and preparing for the danger.

EMILY: Do you feel like being women helped or hindered you as you launched your businesses?

STACEY: Yes.

EMILY: "Yes," both?

STACEY: There are doors that get cracked open just so they can see that you're out there. It doesn't necessarily mean they're going to invite you in. And a lot of women experience this with programs that are geared toward women. And as a woman of color myself, there's never the ability to leave behind the dimension of race when gender is also part of the conversation. Lara and I talk about it in the book: that there have been moments where we've had to confront both pieces, where there are expectations that come along with gender—some that come with race, some that come together—and that the challenge is often trying to understand which ism you're facing. But the opportunity is understanding how you can leverage the diversity and the distinction of who you are to differentiate yourself. So as women in business, we often see problems in a different way. We are used to having to navigate and circumnavigate challenges. The same thing is true for people of color.

Part of what has helped our business relationship is that we bring our different perspectives from gender and these other dimensions into how we problem-solve, because we aren't going to have access to the traditional resources. We're not going to have the standard opportunities that others may take for granted. Our responsibility is to figure out how do we get where we need to be, not despite who we are, but recognizing that what people see isn't going to change even if we close our eyes really tight and hope they don't notice. So, you decide how you're going to leverage it, and you prepare for when it is used against you.

LARA: I would say I've always believed that your greatest strength is also your greatest weakness. And there are times when it's your choice how to use it—meaning the mindset that you approach it with could determine whether that becomes your strength or your weakness.

For example, I am very often, as you can imagine, on panels in the fintech space, where I am the only female. And I would tell people that when I see that situation, I choose for being a female to be my superpower. And I mentally choose that. I mentally say to myself, "I'm the only woman on this panel. That is my superpower." What I mean by that is I'm not going to try to blend in. In fact, it's quite the opposite. I'm probably going to wear a very bright and glaring statement necklace, and I am going to say something boldly that makes the audience uncomfortable, and I'm going to do that because you are going to remember me.

Adapted from "Stacey Abrams and Lara Hodgson on Starting and Scaling a Small Business," Women at Work *podcast, bonus episode, February 21, 2022.*

SECTION TWO

Be Your Own Career Coach

5

What to Do When You Don't Feel Valued at Work

by Rebecca Knight

It's no fun to toil away at a job where your efforts go unnoticed. How can you highlight your achievements without bragging about your work? Who should you talk to about feeling underappreciated? And if the situation doesn't change, how long should you stay?

What the Experts Say

"There's nothing worse than feeling unseen and unheard in the workplace," says Annie McKee, author of *How to Be Happy at Work*. "We all have a human need to be appreciated for our efforts, and so when your colleagues don't notice [your contributions], it makes you feel as though you don't belong." You might also start to worry—justifiably—about your potential professional advancement. "Self-doubt starts to creep in," McKee says, "and you think, 'If no one notices what I'm doing, how am I going to get ahead?'" But you are not powerless to change the situation, says Karen Dillon, author of the *HBR Guide to Office Politics*. "There are many ways to make sure people understand and see what you do." The key, she says, is to find "diplomatic ways to toot your own horn." Here are some ideas.

Be realistic

Before you take any action, ask yourself whether you're being realistic about the amount of appreciation "you expect from your boss, colleagues, peers, and clients," says McKee. "People are very busy. The feedback might not be as much as you want," but it might be reasonable within the context of your organization. "You are dealing with human beings," adds Dillon. "Even with good intentions, your colleagues and manager might overlook what you do and take you for granted." When you're feeling unappreciated, she recommends running a "personal litmus test" on your recent accomplishments. Ask yourself, "Was my work extraordinary? Was it over and above what my peers typically do?" And importantly, "If I had to ask for credit for it, would I sound like a jerk?" If you're unsure, seek a second opinion from a "slightly senior colleague" or a peer you "deeply respect."

Talk to your boss

If your above-par efforts are going unsung, engage your boss in a conversation, says McKee. Granted, this will be easier with some managers than it would be with others. "The average boss doesn't pay attention to human needs," says McKee. If yours falls into that category, keep in mind that "you're not going to change that person, but you can signal that you'd like more dialogue on your performance," she says. "And if your boss is average to good, he might heed the call." Of course, you must be subtle. "Don't go in saying, 'I want more appreciation.'" Instead, McKee recommends saying something along the lines of "I'd like to talk about the past three months and get a sense of where my strengths lie and where I could learn." Come prepared with specific examples, advises Dillon. She suggests drawing up a list of your recent achievements to jog your manager's memory of your good work. "Most managers are happy to have that list," she says.

Increase your team's visibility

If you manage a team, you also need to look for ways to explain to others what the group does and why it's valuable, says Dillon. "In our hectic daily lives, your boss and colleagues might not be aware of" the ins and outs of your job. She advises asking your manager for a sliver of time to "talk about what your team does, what its goals are, and ways you're striving to do better." McKee also suggests subtler ways to draw attention to the group's day-to-day efforts. Don't let presentations or reports go out without making clear who created them. "Make sure everyone's name goes on the work product," she says. You want people beyond your manager to see what your team is delivering. Make sure to spread, not hoard, credit when it's due. But don't be afraid to tout your own leadership. "Sometimes, in your efforts to be inclusive and not sound self-aggrandizing, you miss an opportunity," Dillon explains. Women tend to do this more than men, she notes. It's okay to "use the word *I*, as in 'I accomplished X and Y, and I am grateful for the support that I had.'"

Recognize others' contributions

"Paradoxically," says McKee, one surefire way to get your own work noticed is to "praise and appreciate others. By being the person who notices a job well done, you can be the agent of change" in your organization's culture. Most often the "response from the other person will be to return the favor," she adds. If your boss is not one to dispense positive feedback, talk to your team about how you can better support one another, and generate optimism among the ranks. "Because of the pace of our organizations, what we produce becomes passé or invisible fast," notes McKee. She recommends creating norms in your team so that when a colleague makes an important contribution or finishes a piece of work, "everyone stops for a nanosecond and says yay!" But don't get carried away, cautions Dillon. "Sending extensive thank-yous can diminish the message," she says. "Use your judgment. Ask, 'Who really deserves acknowledgment for going the extra mile?'"

Validate yourself

While being appreciated and valued for your work is a wonderful thing, you can't expect all your "motivation to come from honors, accolades, and public gratitude," says Dillon. Intrinsic motivators are much more powerful. "You need to strive to find meaning in the work itself."

McKee concurs. "Ultimately over the course of your working life, you want to move away from the need for external validation," she says. "Real fulfillment comes from within." She suggests making an effort to pat yourself on the back regularly. "Try to carve out time at the end of each week to reflect on what went well and what didn't go as well." This is a useful exercise for remembering both what you're good at and why you do what you do. "Be careful not to sink into deficiency mode where you [dwell on] everything you did wrong," she adds. "Catalog the wins."

Consider moving on

If you continue to feel undervalued and unappreciated by your company, it might be a sign that it's not the right place for you. "We all stay in jobs that aren't perfect, for a lot of reasons," says McKee. Maybe you need the experience, or perhaps you can't move because you need to be in a certain geographic region for your spouse or partner. But if you've tried to make the job more validating and fulfilling, and nothing has worked, it might be time to look for a new one.

Case Study: Raising Your Profile by Showcasing Your (and Others') Contributions

Anna Brockway started her career as a junior account executive at a large ad agency in San Francisco.

She loved her job and her main client, Levi Strauss, and she worked incredibly hard. Still, it was difficult to stand out among her peers, and she often felt that her efforts went unnoticed. "I was spending extra hours developing new programs and ideas for [my client], but the work was getting lost in the sea of projects already in flight," she recalls. "I was struggling with how to get my work to be more visible so I could be more appreciated."

On reflection, Brockway realizes that many young women tend to wait for recognition rather than seeking it. "I think we're taught implicitly or explicitly to be demure," she says. "Showcasing your work is like running an internal PR campaign. You don't want to gloat, but you also don't want to be invisible."

One day, Brockway saw a colleague make a client presentation about a new idea and realized that transparency was the key. "It wasn't that the client didn't care," she explains. "They just didn't know what I was doing!"

Brockway developed a simple 15-minute description of all the work she'd done to help the company better showcase its newest products on the front aisle of stores. This summary highlighted not only her own efforts but also those of the Levi Strauss designers, who had recently added new finishes and fits and "were seeking a way to get their work noticed too."

"I remember the head merchant saying how honored he was" to be included in the presentation and thanked for his own work.

Two years later, Levi Strauss brought Brockway in house, and she later became the head of its worldwide marketing group.

Today she is the cofounder and chief marketing officer of Chairish, the online marketplace for vintage decor, furniture, and art. Every Monday at 2 p.m., she writes a personal "good, old-fashioned" thank you note to one of her team members. "I believe people feel most valued by recognition," she says. "Money, promotions, and more are really nice, but personal validation is the most meaningful."

Adapted from content posted on hbr.org, December 26, 2017 (product #H0433N).

6

Early Career Advice We Could All Benefit From

A conversation with Paige Cohen

"How do I balance assertiveness and persuasion?" "How do I set myself up now if I want to be CEO someday?" These are just a few of the common workplace questions that younger women ask themselves when they're starting off their careers. Knowing the answers to these questions early in their careers sets folks up for success. And for those whose early career feels like a distant memory, you could benefit from reading this chapter to refresh your thinking and to revel in a moment of pride—remind yourself how far you've come, even on those days when you feel as though you're not where you want to be.

Paige Cohen, editor of HBR Ascend, joins Amy Bernstein to share their experience and answer questions from listeners early in their careers who are looking for advice on their workplace quandaries.

Balancing Assertiveness with Persuasion

PAIGE COHEN: Let's start off with a question written in response to a podcast episode that *Women at Work* published: "Too Shy to Be a Leader." This person says she's outgoing in life, but when it comes to work, she's shy, quiet, and more introverted. And this is usually because she's questioning her own competency or the value of what she has to contribute at work. Another recurring pattern she has noticed is that in performance reviews, she'll often get feedback that says she needs to be more assertive. She wrote, "Granted, I'm sure there's always opportunity to be more assertive as a woman, but I'd like to think too much assertiveness could also be a point of criticism." And she says that she wants to find a balance between assertiveness and persuasion. What are our thoughts on this?

AMY BERNSTEIN: This is the famous double bind that women face in the workplace and have faced since there have been women in the workplace. There's that great article "How Women Manage the Gendered Norms of Leadership," by Wei Zheng, Ronit Kark and Alyson Meister, that points out the four kinds of tensions, the balancing act that women have to perform in the workplace. You know, you have to be demanding but caring. You have to be authoritative yet participative. All of that stuff. Haven't you felt that?

PAIGE: Yes, I definitely have. I found this letter super relatable, even though I wouldn't say I'm an extroverted person in real life or at work. But especially in my first couple of jobs, I was very quiet at work, and I found it difficult to advocate for myself. And then when I did, I almost felt like I was being gaslit by my manager or by HR, that I was being told I was bossy, or that I was just bothering people or being unreasonable. And it was so hard to deal with, because as a young person in the workplace, everybody wants to be liked. So, if you feel like you're being bossy or annoying people by asking for what you want, it's tempting to just shut down and be quiet. Is this something you've ever faced throughout your career?

AMY: Oh my God, of course . . . But you've navigated this more recently than I. How did you do it? It must be very fresh for you.

PAIGE: Yeah, definitely, for me it's been building up confidence by leaning on my strengths. I'm more of a quiet and shy person naturally. What I'll do, if there's a meeting I care about, and I know I want to speak up—it's an important topic—I might just practice beforehand what I want to say, which can seem tedious but is helpful when you finally raise your hand, to have rehearsed it a little bit.

AMY: I agree with that. It's super tedious. But when you're in that presentation, and you know it cold, it gives you so much more confidence.

PAIGE: I thought this idea of persuasion that she's talking about, like mixing the two, assertiveness and persuasion, is something I've had to navigate a lot, especially when it comes to winning over maybe more senior employees at new roles. I've found that I've had to act small before I can act big around someone.

AMY: Say more about that. Give us an example.

PAIGE: When I first started working at HBR, I made this multimedia video, for one of our sub-brands, and a person who was much more senior than me gave me a long page of feedback. Some of it was really helpful, but some of it was about them asserting their authority over me like, "This is my thing." So, before I could do what I wanted to do, I had to be overly verbal and say, "Thank you so much for this feedback. I think it's so important that you give this to me, and that I'm able to see it from all these perspectives. This is going to help make the video so much better." And I never had to deal with it from that person again, because they were like, "Oh this person appreciates me, and this person trusts my feedback." And that way I could start taking it in my own direction, and it was easier. And that was a more persuasive way of being assertive than an outright way of being assertive, I would say.

AMY: Most people in that situation would have taken that personally and might have even shut down after receiving a page of feedback. And you read it for what it was. That's kind of amazing.

PAIGE: I come from a background of film school and creative writing, and you're just constantly, constantly getting feedback from people. Sometimes people take your story personally. Sometimes people take your work personally. After a while, it becomes emotionally trying to think too much about anything beyond, "the work is the work." If you're afraid to be assertive, or if you're doubting yourself at work, it's helpful to draw those boundaries, and it's empowering to say, my work is my work. Something about that separation helps it be not as big of a deal. So, you go in, you do your thing, and you leave. If you don't overthink it, you might find that some of that questioning of your own competency or your value goes away if you're able to just have those boundaries.

AMY: I totally know what you're talking about, and I think some of what I take from what you're saying is that it's important to sort of strip away the personal and try to take the real value. And I think that when you're trying to overcome your own shyness, and when you're trying to become more assertive, and you're worried about crossing that line, you know, not making that balance, not being able to handle that balance, I think that there's something in what you're saying right now about not taking things personally, trying to see the situation for what it is. But also, you have to have confidence to do that.

PAIGE: Yeah. And you could start by just reading the room. And start small and see how you feel afterward. And you'll get more and more comfortable with it. Compared to where I was at the beginning of my career, to how much more comfortable I am being assertive now, it's just all through those little moments of practice. And having allies and a network of women who will reassure you and be your champions, it's super helpful just to get out of your own head. You kind of need someone sometimes. Nicole, who used to be a host at *Women at Work*, and I used to do this for each other all the time. After a meeting, we'd say, "Was what I said OK? What did you think of that? Did that sound good?" And it was just helpful to have that ally in your corner.

AMY: Yeah, and to understand that it's that thing about asking yourself, what the worst is that could happen, if you assert yourself. I mean, if someone disagrees with you, big deal. Someone disagrees with you.

Setting Yourself Up for the C-Suite

PAIGE: This question is from a 25-year-old woman. She works in the veterinary marketing industry. She asks, "I am working on aligning myself to be in a C-suite position one day. Do you have any tips for how to set myself up for success?" I'm curious what your first reaction is, Amy, given that you're a badass boss at HBR and have been in so many leadership roles, and even VP roles in the past.

AMY: The first thing I noticed about her is her ambition, and I salute her ambition. Aim high. That is the only way to get to the top, right? The most fundamental thing I can say here is, don't lose sight of the job you're supposed to do, but look for every single opportunity you can find to demonstrate your ability to do additional work, your ambition, your willingness to learn. It's the difference between coming across as kind of a jerk and coming across as the teammate everyone wants to work with. You know what I mean?

PAIGE: Yeah, definitely. This question really makes me think of an article that one of the *Women at Work* hosts, Amy Gallo, wrote: "Act Like a Leader Before You Are One." You want to make your teammates and your boss look good.

AMY: One of the things that Amy [Gallo] says that I think is so totally true is, don't overstate your expertise. Don't exert authority where you don't have any, is what she writes. She says, use your influence to demonstrate your leadership chops. I think that is so important. That's that thing about not being a jerk.

PAIGE: At HBR, I've experienced this a little bit coming into a role. I came in as an associate editor, and I'm in a senior editor role now. I think a part of being able to grow here has been another piece of Amy's advice and something that touches on, I think, my relationship with you is, networking and finding role models in people who are in positions that you admire and asking them how they got there and what you can do. It kind of goes back to some of those conversations you and I have had throughout my three years here.

AMY: Anna Ranieri also wrote something for us that touches on that. She points out that if you want to get somewhere, you have to figure out what skills you'll need, and that's what a lot of the conversations you and I have had have been about. You wanted to know what was required of the next step. And then you wanted to figure out how to both acquire those skills and demonstrate them. You seem to have a kind of intuitive sense about that. But it worked, look where you are. It didn't take very long.

PAIGE: I also applaud this person for their ambition, because I definitely was not at that place when I was 25 years old. I still don't want to be in the C-suite. It seems like way too much responsibility. But I think it's amazing that this person's already thinking about it.

Adapted from "We Answer Questions from Early Career Listeners," Women at Work *podcast, bonus episode, December 21, 2020.*

7

How to Ask for the Job Title You Deserve

by Rebecca Knight

Your job title isn't everything—but it does matter. When you're offered a new role or have been in the same position for some time, how should you think about what title you deserve? How do you decide whether it's worth negotiating? If you don't think you can get a raise, should you even ask for a change in your title? And what about the other side of the coin: How should you respond if your boss offers you a promotion in title—with no raise?

What the Experts Say

When accepting a new position or angling for a promotion, most people tend to focus on salary negotiation. But your job title should also be part of the equation, says Margaret

Neale, professor at Stanford Graduate School of Business and coauthor of *Getting (More of) What You Want*. It's "a signal both to the outside world and to your colleagues of what level you are within your organization," she says, explaining that your title should be seen as part of "your compensation package," an element that affords status and connections and can "help you do your job better." Your title can also have a big impact on your day-to-day happiness and engagement, says Dan Cable, professor at London Business School. "It is a form of self-expression in the workplace," he says. "It is a symbolic representation of what you do and the value that you bring." So, whether you're eyeing a new role or a new title in your current one, here are some ideas for how to go about it.

Reflect

Negotiating or renegotiating your title requires a bit of soul-searching. Why do you want a certain title? And why do you think you deserve it? These are things you need to think through to figure out if you should even make the request. If you've been at your company awhile, "it may be that your scope and responsibilities have expanded but your title is the same, and you're still being paid a level below what you're currently doing," Neale says. In that case, a discussion with your boss is probably justified. Or perhaps you're mulling over new opportunities and want to put yourself in a better position, since prospective employers might use your title as an indicator of how much money you earn. "At a time when companies are less able to ask and people are less willing to share their compensation history, your title is a way for future employers to triangulate your expectations," she explains. And if you've been offered a position at another company, negotiating your title could be a way to tweak your job responsibilities to do more of what you love, Cable says. "Think of it as an opportunity to customize the role more to your skills and interests."

Do your homework

The second step involves identifying a specific title that accurately reflects your expertise, responsibilities, and status in the organization. Use resources like LinkedIn and Glassdoor to look at the titles of peers at different companies. In addition, Cable says, consider what job title would make you feel the most valued and empowered. "Think about why you're effective," he says. For instance, imagine that you're a senior analyst at a large consultancy "but what you're really good at is visual presentations involving data. In this case, you might ask for 'client artist' to be added to your title, because that's the area where you shine." At the same time, you must be mindful of what's realistic within the context of your firm and industry, Neale says. "In every organization there is a hierarchy. And your title needs to provide information about your level within [it].” If you’re planning to ask for an “avant-garde title,” she recommends that you “make sure you have a more traditional equivalent.” For instance, if you ask for the title of *chief motivational officer*, your business card might spell out that you’re also “EVP, Human Resource Planning.”

Think holistically

Next, you need to prioritize. Compared with salary, bonuses, job responsibilities, vacation time, and work schedule, how much should you emphasize your desired title as you negotiate your package? “I strongly counsel against single-issue negotiations,” Neale says. “Your title should be part of a multi-issue discussion. So think about all the resources you need to do your job better.” Whether you’re changing jobs or you’ve been at the same organization for years, ask yourself, “Which benefits will be most important?” If title is one of them, proceed.

Listen first . . .

The most important thing you can do to prepare for the negotiation with your current or prospective manager is to listen. “During your job interviews,” Neale says, “you should be sensitive to what people are telling you about the challenges that the organization faces. . . . If you’re already inside, you should know what they are.” Try to understand what your superiors care about most and what really worries them, so you can build your case around that. "People are most influenced by their own words and perspectives," Neale explains. "Don't be so focused on what you want that you don't hear what your boss wants."

. . . Strategize second

When preparing your pitch, ask yourself one question: "What would make this person say yes?" Neale recommends looking at it this way: "Think, 'Which of my boss's problems would my promotion solve?'" If you don't know, you're not ready for the conversation. It helps to "have a reason to ask," she adds. Perhaps you just inked a big new deal, executed an important project, or have been offered another job but want to stay at your organization. You'll also need to make the case that a new title will help you be more efficient and effective in your job, perhaps by giving you added gravitas or credibility. Cable notes that some job titles—particularly personalized ones—"help you build rapport with clients and colleagues." They "open the door for other people to ask questions about what you do in a unique and personal way," he says. "That can be really valuable in building authentic and sincere relationships."

Talk to your boss

When the time comes to broach the subject with your boss, Cable recommends coming at the conversation from "a learning mode." For applicants, "this is a chance to talk about what you can bring to the job" and learn more about how the hiring manager defines success in the role. "You might say, 'I see that the current job title is "Analyst," which is fairly generic. If you could rename this title, what might better reflect the role?'" This question, he says, "often leads to a very good, very real conversation." If you're already at the organization and would like a new title, Cable recommends showing your boss some research that points to the power of job titles to energize workers and boost morale. "Some bosses are rigid and will have an over-my-dead-body response. But others might see the issue as timely and interesting and a way to allow their employees more self-expression." Whatever you do, don't be a demanding prima donna. Project your strength but also your modesty. Neale suggests highlighting "the solutions that you provide to your boss" and the "skills and abilities you're using to move the organization forward."

Be appreciative (to a point)

If your manager agrees to your desired title (or some version of it), your first response should be "thank you." If you're disappointed that it comes with no other new benefits, remember that it's not necessarily a one-and-done deal, Neale says. "It's an ongoing negotiation." So, she advises, "take the opportunity in the nicest way possible to clue him in to the fact that, while you're appreciative, it's not enough, and you will be back." If you are shut down completely—given no change in title, pay, or any other perk—she suggests asking your boss to provide more detail about the criteria that you're being judged on and how you'll both know that you've "achieved those metrics." Essentially, the question is, "What would it take to advance?"

Case Study: Keeping Negotiation for Your Compensation Package Open

After Rhonda Rees graduated from college, she landed an entry-level job at a small public relations firm in the Los Angeles area. "My job title was PR assistant," she recalls. "I was green, and because it was an entry-level position, nobody had any real expectations of me."

Rees was determined to absorb everything she could about the PR business. She viewed her boss—we'll call him George—as a mentor. George saw Rees's potential and gave her an increasing amount of work and responsibility. "A lot got dropped in my lap," she says.

But she wasn't bitter about it; rather, she was eager to prove herself. "I discovered I had a knack for bringing in business because I loved cold-calling," she says. "It wasn't long before I started bringing in the bread-and-butter clients."

George was pleased with Rees's work—and he told her so. "It was his idea to put me on commission," she says.

"In addition to my salary, I got 10% in commission, and I was content with that. I just kept doing what I was doing."

As other employees moved on to other jobs and George spent more and more time on the golf course, Rees's workload increased further. And yet because she was still just a PR assistant, she had to work even harder for clients to take her seriously.

She eventually realized she needed a title to match the role she played. "At first I thought I was doing the job of an account executive, but then suddenly I was doing the job of an account supervisor," she says. "I remember thinking that George considered me to be that informally, but I still didn't have the title."

She decided to talk to him. "I went into his office and explained all that I was doing and said that I had become pretty indispensable to the business. I asked for a raise and to be made an account supervisor," she says.

"He actually surprised me and gave me the title of VP. I still had the same duties as before, but with the new title and a small raise."

Rees thanked George. She says she was "content" for a little while after that, but she soon decided she wanted more out of her career. "The experience gave me the confidence to open up my own business," she says. "And so I did. I knew I could run the show. Now I'm the boss and call myself president."

Adapted from content posted on hbr.org, July 17, 2017 (product #H03SBZ).

8

Get Comfortable Playing Office Politics

by Lisa Zigarmi, Julie Diamond, and Lesli Mones

By now, it's a tired refrain: Women, particularly women of color, are significantly outnumbered at the senior leadership level in organizations.

The causes of the leadership gender gap are numerous, as are its proposed solutions. One area of research points to differences concerning women's response to office politics. Politics, broadly defined as the ability to successfully navigate the unwritten rules of how things get done and through whom, includes understanding the motivations of others and using this knowledge to enhance one's personal interest and organizational objectives.

In our experience as psychologists and coaches, we have found that many women have an averse, almost allergic reaction, to office politics. Numerous studies confirm this attitude; women tend to see it as something dirty or dishonest and as a stressful aspect that reduces their job satisfaction.

And yet, by nature, humans are relational beings. Political skill matters; it is a necessary part of organizational life. Studies affirm that good political skills are critical to career advancement.

We recognize that engaging in office politics can be stressful. It often forces people to stretch beyond their natural preferences and patterns. We aim to help you participate in politics in ways that reduce discomfort and maximize career advancement.

This chapter identifies some commonly held beliefs underlying women's aversion to being political at work. Next, it offers mindset shifts that have helped hundreds of women use political skills to their advantage.

Five Reasons Women Dislike Office Politics

What justification have you given for avoiding office politics? No doubt you have told yourself or others why politics is not your game or have heard colleagues explain their reasons for staying out of the political fray. Let's walk through five common reasons women avoid office politics.

My work should speak for itself

Being political contradicts many people's belief in meritocracy. The notion that one has to do more than excel at work itself is anathema to most working people. However, for women and other marginalized groups, who often have to work twice as hard to counter the bias related to their gender and race, the importance of political skills can be experienced as an even greater insult and burden.

Building connections is an extracurricular activity

Cultivating political relationships often feels extraneous and distracting from the work, like just another item on a to-do list. And for women, who spend on average 37% more time than men do on housework and chores in addition to their full-time jobs (not to mention the non-promotable office "housework" discussed in chapter 9), the idea that women have to find more space and time for these additional activities feels unreasonable.[1]

It's inauthentic

Politics is often seen as posturing, making alliances with those who have clout or supporting initiatives that are popular, simply for the sake of staying close to the power source. To many, these actions can feel inauthentic and, at times, duplicitous.

I don't like playing hardball

Office politics often plays out as a zero-sum game, involving gossip, backstabbing, sabotaging, and even intimidation.

Women and a fair number of men have an aversion to these tactics and prefer power that is based on influence, relationships, and win-win approaches.

The penalties are too great

Women are penalized for displaying political skill. Studies show that women are judged more harshly for being assertive or competitive, two common characteristics of office politics.[2] And, consequently, they are penalized for it.

Do you hold any of these beliefs? If so, it's an understandable attitude. There's validity to these beliefs. And yet, if you don't challenge them, you may be limiting your potential. In our work, we have found that cultivating the following five mindsets is an effective way to help counter these beliefs and embrace and develop political skills.

Five Ways to Shift Your Mindset Around Playing Politics

From "My work should speak for itself" to "It's my responsibility to show people how my work connects to theirs"

No one is an island. When people believe their work should speak for itself, they fail to recognize the interdependence of organizational life. Believing your work should speak for itself is a narrow, functional view of a job; you assume that others can fully appreciate and comprehend the part you play in the larger organizational puzzle.

We typically see this belief in two groups. The first is from very technical leaders—those with a highly valued, specialized area of expertise. It's easy for these experts to see how the organization depends on what *they* provide, but it's less obvious to them how their work depends on others.

We also have heard this response from those who are more comfortable with a hierarchical style of leadership and who have a more deferential relationship with management. They question the necessity of advocating for themselves, considering it the task of their manager to see and evaluate their performance.

When we work with people on shifting away from this mindset, we focus on moving from a functional or expert mindset to an enterprise one, an attitude that enables people to connect their area of expertise to the larger business needs. With an enterprise mindset, people think in terms of what's best for the whole organization, not just their small part of it.

One of us coached a senior executive who rose rapidly through the ranks from director to vice president in a very technical, male-dominated field. She navigated the politics in her rise to the top by learning how to connect her own work to that of others. Before every conversation, every meeting, and every presentation, she would take five minutes to anticipate the possible blowback or resistance she could incur. She took a careful inventory of her audience, considering who they were, what their needs were, and the priorities they were facing. She would then consider ways to connect her contributions to their needs, positioning herself as a necessary and intrinsic part of everyone else's success. By carefully tying her work to others and to the organization's goals, she tied her success to the success of others, thereby ensuring that they saw the value in what she had to offer.

From "Building connections is an extracurricular activity" to "Building connections is a force multiplier"

Work gets done with and through people. And the higher up you go, the more this is true. In the interdependent world of work, where you need others to help you accomplish your goals, you must continuously nurture relationships and learn from others to succeed.

For example, attending a women's conference can double a woman's likelihood of receiving a promotion within a year, triple the likelihood of a more than 10% pay increase within a year, and increase her sense of optimism by up to 78%, immediately.[3] Something powerful happens when people engage with others. They become more inspired. They learn new strategies for career advancement. They are exposed to new ideas. They build confidence in asking for what they need and maybe even find a way to share their wisdom with others.

When we help leaders move away from this mindset, we help them see the benefits, not just the burden, of making connections. We host six-month leadership development programs in organizations where participants can meet, repeatedly, as cohorts. Women who are seeking new opportunities, who are stuck in their career trajectory, or who are struggling with leadership conflicts find it productive to hear from others in similar positions. They can learn new approaches for promoting themselves and discover alternatives for managing their challenges.

In the final session, participants give a five-minute presentation on a topic that has big career implications after rehearsing and revising their presentations in small groups. These dress rehearsals give people the opportunity to hone their stories, more clearly articulate their facts, and bolster their stage presence for maximum effectiveness. Countless participants credit the feedback from their new network with helping them adjust and sharpen their presentations to the point that they ultimately land funding, drive new strategy, and galvanize followers. In several instances, the women also helped each other find new roles, make the transition into different departments, and gain access into new and influential networks. The relationships built in the program and the perspectives gathered from those relationships help our participants amplify their impact.

From "It's inauthentic" to "I'm being paid to have a point of view and share it"

Research shows that authenticity requires two things: conscious awareness (knowing who you are, your motives, and what you're bringing to the current situation) and expression (consciously aligning your behavior with your awareness).[4] It means acting in accordance with your true feelings, thoughts, and highest intentions in a way that serves the circumstances. Authenticity requires discernment, courage, and self-determination. It's not a reaction to what's happening around you; it's relating to the players and situation from a grounded sense of who you are.

You're more negatively affected by office politics if you don't know what you stand for or don't have the courage to advocate for it. To be political—and authentic—you must know what your values and intentions are so that you can move projects and teams forward in a way that aligns with you and the organization's goals. In some ways, it's easier for people to be against politics than it is to get clear on what they stand for and champion it.

When we help people move away from the belief that politics is inauthentic, we help them discern their purpose and values so they can make choices that reflect these principles. One of us coached a woman who was discouraged by the leadership behavior of the senior leaders in her business unit. As a result, rather than seeking promotion to the next level, she was considering quitting. Through coaching, she realized that her decision was a reaction to her colleagues' behavior, yet she hadn't defined the leadership behavior she valued. After we helped her clarify her own leadership point of view, she felt inspired to model new behaviors and open up conversations inside her business unit about the role leaders play in creating the culture. This new approach changed her attitude toward her current job, and she felt more motivated to stay in the role and even to apply for a promotion. Rather than reacting to what she disliked, she made a conscious decision to be a role model for the leadership behavior she wanted to see present in her organization.

From "I don't like playing hardball" to "My leadership tactic needs to match the situation"

Political behavior can be a turnoff, especially when it involves hard-power tactics such as coercion, intimidation, and sabotage. For many people, no matter their gender, the use of such forcible pressure is what being political means, as opposed to using softer-power tactics of persuasion, building alliances, and offering assistance.

Yet power, hard or soft, is neither good nor bad. What makes it beneficial or harmful is the motivation behind its use and the impact it has on others. While we can easily see the negative applications of hard power, soft power can also be misused, or used to nefarious ends. Consider how Bernie Madoff, Jeffrey Skilling, and Jim Jones employed persuasion, charisma, and relationship building.

To encourage our clients not to view power tactics as necessarily bad, we help them understand that their application of hard or soft power tactics should be situational, not a matter of preference or style. Some situations call for hard power, and some for soft power. Specifically, we may need to use hard-power tactics to hold people accountable, make tough and unpopular decisions, set boundaries, or enact consequences to inappropriate workplace behavior.

One of us coached a leader who had a decided preference for soft-power tactics. She worked in a creative industry in which her collaborative style worked well at first. But within a few months of her leading a new team, team members began to complain about burnout. Shortly thereafter, a few senior team members quit because of conflict. These developments led her to look at the dynamics on the team and her own leadership.

Through discussions with each team member, she realized that her collaborative approach had allowed team meetings to be dominated and derailed by a few vocal members. Agendas were often hijacked by tangential discussions, and meetings often ended without clarity or direction, forcing people to spend hours in discussion to recap and rehash the outcomes.

Our client learned to incorporate hard-power tactics to match the team dynamic. She began to intervene, set boundaries, create rules for conversation, and hold people accountable if they failed to follow the meeting guidelines. It was a revelation to her to realize that collaborative leadership had its limits and that harder-power tactics can also have a place.

From "The penalties are too great" to "I prioritize my growth"

Women are often penalized for being ambitious and displaying political skill. Along with minorities, women pay a steep price for displaying ambition. The research is clear: Negative stereotypes have negative consequences for one's career.[5]

And yet, for many, the alternative may be worse. While the blowback to displaying ambition is tough, so too is the personal and psychological toll of not striving to fulfill your potential and not stretching to reach your goals. For many women and minorities, waiting for the world to change before they can assert themselves is a steeper price to pay than the backlash of being ambitious.

The mindset here is one of prioritizing growth. But this shouldn't be done naively. You must be prepared for the consequences you may face. You may need to gather resources and allies and ensure you have the support in your personal and professional life before undertaking any action. And above all, you'll want to have a plan B or even a plan C in place. Consider, realistically, the penalties you may face. Do you have alternatives in mind if things don't work out as planned? Are you prepared to switch business units or even companies if necessary?

A growth mindset (the belief that talents can be developed through hard work, good strategies, and input from others) is protective against negative stereotypes. For example, one study found that when Black university students were taught to have a growth mindset, they were less likely to internalize the negative stereotype directed at them and thus had better outcomes in their studies.[6] On the other hand, students with a fixed mindset, seeing themselves as unable to change, were more prone to suffer the effects of the negative stereotyping.

One of us coached a woman who described her manager as someone who stifled her ambition, denied her access to senior leaders, and routinely took credit for her work. She felt pushed out by her manager and saw no option but to leave the firm. Through coaching, she realized that she had in fact mastered her role. There wasn't room to learn new skills, create more impact, or meet new stakeholders. Her lack of opportunity had as much to do with her role's limited scope as it had to do with her disparaging manager.

By recognizing her need for growth, she decided to intentionally seek a new role with more scope and impact potential outside her firm. Rather than feeling chased out, she realized it was her old position, more than her leader, that was limiting her career. This mindset shift made her the hero of the story instead of the victim.

The harsh reality is that women and racialized minorities face discrimination, negative stereotypes, and other types of hostility. But there are choices to be made, choices that provide more flexibility and resilience, or less. Preparing yourself, gathering allies and resources, having a plan B in place, and developing a growth mindset that frames the challenge as an opportunity to learn and grow can be powerful protection for the backlash you may face.

. . .

Office politics impacts your work experience and your projects, whether you participate in it or not. We argue that it's better to be a player than a pawn. The women we coach want to be leading at the highest levels, and yet many have not examined their limiting beliefs about using political skills to advance their careers. The mindset you bring to any situation, whether it is negative or positive, can impede or promote your success.

As a reader, did you notice yourself agreeing with any of the limiting beliefs outlined in this chapter? If so, can you see a way to shift your mindset to one that gives you more power over your experience and possibilities in your career?

Office politics matters because we are relational beings; getting ahead is as much about people and relationships as it is about skills and experience. Your ability to participate in politics and to employ your political skills is not just critical to career advancement but equally important for your overall well-being at work.

Adapted from "How Women Can Get Comfortable 'Playing Politics' at Work," on hbr.org, January 19, 2022 (product #H06T5D).

9

Are You Taking On Too Many Non-Promotable Tasks?

by Linda Babcock, Brenda Peyser, Lise Vesterlund, and Laurie R. Weingart

Francesca, a third-year associate at a prestigious law firm (and a young woman we know), loved her job. When her boss asked her to help run the summer intern program, she immediately said yes. It was a chance for her to learn about different departments, meet partners, and showcase her organizational skills. She put a lot of time and energy into it. But once performance reviews rolled around three years later, her efforts were never mentioned. Instead, her boss warned Francesca that her billable hours had fallen behind. She was baffled and disappointed—what she thought would benefit her career didn't seem to matter at all.

Does this situation sound familiar? We're not surprised.

Like Francesca, many workers we've encountered during the research for our book *The No Club: Putting a Stop to Women's Dead-End Work*, devote excessive hours to tasks that help their organizations, but the tasks do nothing to advance their careers. These are known as non-promotable tasks (NPTs), or unrewarded responsibilities. Maybe you're the person who trains new hires, takes notes at a meeting, organizes the holiday party, fills in for absent colleagues, or handles that low-revenue and time-consuming client. Everyone benefits when these NPTs get done. But sadly, and too often, the person who does them ends up robbed of valuable time and the promotable work that actually grows paychecks and careers.

Our research shows that this problem is particularly pernicious for women. We asked the management team at a professional services firm to rank work assignments by how promotable they were and then examined how employees spent their time. We found that, independent of rank, the median female employee spent 200 more hours per year on non-promotable work than her male counterparts. To put that into perspective, women spent an additional month on dead-end assignments.

Further, in a controlled setting where men and women were equally good at executing NPTs, we found that women were handling a greater number of them—not because of preference or attitude—but because they were *expected* to say yes more often.[1] As a result, women were asked and volunteered to do NPTs frequently, while men often got a free pass.

These observations show why, especially for women, understanding what assignments are non-promotable, the consequences of taking them on, and the reasons you might feel pressure to say yes can help you steer clear of Francesca's mistake.

How to Identify Non-Promotable Tasks (NPTs)

NPTs have several characteristics that make them recognizable.

NPTs are not instrumental to your organization's mission

All organizations have goals and objectives, and people value some of these aims more than they value others. The less a task aligns with those objectives, the lower its promotability. For Francesca, serving clients is her organization's mission, meaning anything that takes time away from that, like administering the summer intern program, is likely to be non-promotable. Francesca's performance evaluation was less stellar than she wanted because she spent too much time on a task that wasn't directly connected to the bottom line.

NPTs are often not visible to others

Less visible tasks tend to be non-promotable because other people cannot see your efforts or impact. NPTs are often done in support of the team's work in a way that can't be credited to you—like editing your coworker's section of the report or making the team's presentations "look pretty." Only Francesca's boss knew about her work on the summer intern program. It was invisible to everyone else.

NPTs may not require specialized skills, and many people can do them

Promotable tasks leverage the unique skills you were hired for; NPTs do not. Gathering résumés, scheduling appointments, and compiling interviewers' notes are tasks Francesca took on that almost anyone in the firm could have performed. None of these tasks relied on her legal knowledge or abilities.

Why We Feel Pressured to Say Yes

There are several reasons why we sometimes feel pressured to say yes, even when we don't have to. Here are some patterns we have observed in our research.

You think you need to decide immediately

We often feel the urgency of a request, even more so if it comes from someone more powerful or higher up in the organization than ourselves. For instance, let's say you bump into your boss in the hallway, and they ask you to take on a task. You may think you need to respond then and there—but you don't have to give an immediate answer.

Rather than automatically saying yes, buy time to gather information, evaluate the task, and think about your career objectives and what you need to do to get there. Here's a rule we use for ourselves: Wait at least 24 hours before saying yes. Instead of "sure," tell the requester, "Thanks so much for thinking of me for this. I need some time to think about it and how it fits in with my other priorities. I'll get back to you by the end of day tomorrow." That will make it easier to say no later.

You have internalized the expectation that you should say yes

Recognize that your discomfort and reluctance to say no (when you are asked once again to take one for the team) likely stems from your internalizing others' expectations of you. This is especially true for women, who may say yes to an NPT to avoid feeling guilty about failing to live up to these expectations.

The next time you are asked to volunteer, ask yourself if doing this task is the best use of your time. If the answer is no, then sit back and let someone else come forward, or better yet, propose that the task be randomly assigned or that everyone take turns doing the work.

You are flattered to be asked

When you feel honored to have been asked, it's hard to see the downside. Francesca said yes because she felt good that her boss had noticed her abilities.

While it's nice to be called on, that positive feeling will quickly disappear once you become buried in the actual work. And if the task is mostly invisible—like organizing an internship program—it will provide no tangible upside. Remember, you can still feel flattered that you were asked, even if you decline the request.

How to Weigh an Opportunity

The next time you're asked to do an NPT, give yourself some time, and use it to carefully evaluate the consequences of taking on the work. Be cognizant of the mistakes you might make when deciding whether to say yes or no.

Consider the implicit no of saying yes

When you take on a new NPT, you will have less time to do something else. When you agree to help another team streamline its workflow, you are implicitly saying no to another activity you could do in that time. If, for example, you miss out on helping your own team with a new product launch, then the opportunity cost of helping someone else do their job can be high. Francesca's implicit no was her billable work. By adding the intern program, she had to cut back on her client hours, which hurt her performance review.

Weigh the urgency of the task

A task with a short deadline will trump a task with a longer one, no matter how insignificant it is. The big tasks such as recruiting new clients may not be very time sensitive, so taking on an NPT or two with short time horizons is likely to put off longer-term initiatives that are more valued by your organization.

Remember that you will also be busy in the future

Three months out, your calendar looks clear, so today's yes doesn't seem so bad. But chances are that your current rush of activity will be the same three months from now. Before you say yes, imagine instead that this distant request is for next week. Would you be as excited to plan the office party next week with your current workload? Probably not!

Evaluate the indirect benefits of the NPT

Not all NPTs are the same. Be intentional in choosing those that are best for you. Some NPTs can help you later. We call these tasks *indirectly promotable*—they might help you gain knowledge, develop skills, or make connections that you can leverage later on. Other NPTs are attractive because they align with your personal mission, like advancing diversity, equity, and inclusion initiatives. In addition to considering the cost of taking on the task, be sure to assess its potential benefits. Knowing that most of us will have to do an NPT from time to time, try to choose the ones that are best for you.

Your road to success will be shorter if you recognize and steer toward the assignments that matter most for your career. You'll be surprised by the recognition you will receive when you finally have the time for the work that is valued most by your organization.

Adapted from content posted on Ascend, hbr.org, April 26, 2022.

10

When Being Indispensable Backfires

by Mita Mallick

A mentor once said to me, "The critical mistake you made is that you became indispensable." "That's why you can't get off his team and move on to your next assignment."

After more than four years in the same role, I found that my career had stalled even though I had gone above and beyond my job description. My boss frequently volunteered my time to other leaders to build their strategy decks. He asked me to call vendors to ask them to purchase annual gala tables for the nonprofit board he served on. He had me write his speeches for external events. He asked me to help manage his LinkedIn profile, and soon other leaders came to me with similar requests. Finally, he asked me to help the CEO and other executives prepare for interviews, because I was so good at crafting media briefs.

The observation from my mentor was a rude awakening. Because I had said yes to every assignment, in hopes that my assistance would help me move on to my next opportunity, I had become indispensable and my manager wouldn't let me go. Being indispensable had temporarily killed my career.

While job-hoppers can be viewed as unreliable or lacking commitment, those who have stayed too long in a role can be perceived as stagnant, too comfortable, and not innovative. Staying in the same role too long can also affect your confidence and your own view of your capabilities. Ultimately, it can stand in the way of your career growth and advancement. Here are four ways to ensure that your career progress doesn't stall.

Make yourself less available

While we're taught that our jobs are to make our managers' jobs easier, that doesn't mean we need to be available 24/7. Living in an always-on attention economy can compel us to always be available to do whatever is needed. I routinely responded to texts at 6:30 a.m. and phone calls at 11 p.m. on Saturdays. I would drop everything when my manager called, even responding to his requests during vacations with my family.

"If you repeatedly respond to texts at 6:30 a.m., your manager expects that you will be available then, because you didn't set your boundaries," Christy DeSantis, founder and chief confidence officer of Fiducia Coaching, told me. "We all need to train our managers on when we are available and when we are not. Make yourself available and present for the career moments that matter. And remember, managers don't always need or expect a response right away, so stop yourself from immediately responding."

In addition to following Christy's advice, focus on being intentional and making an impact during reasonable working hours. Of course, the occasional fire drill and urgent tasks will happen, but retrain your manager on your general availability while continuing to demonstrate your value and expertise.

Say no, and then say yes

Saying no doesn't have to hurt your career. If you're asked to lead the team offsite every quarter, it's time to decline. Say no, then position the no as an opportunity for someone else to lead and learn from the work. Nominate other people who could benefit from taking over the task. If your manager insists that you have to keep doing the work, be explicit about other initiatives or projects you'll have to stop working on to make time for it. Be clear that you're committed to delivering strong work and want to ensure that you aren't being spread too thin.

When you say no, think of something else you would be comfortable taking on and excited to say yes to. Prioritize projects that are important and timely and that give you exposure to the wider organization. Before your manager assigns you work, be proactive and raise your hand for projects that can increase your visibility internally. If you've become indispensable to your manager, saying yes to work that gives you access to other leaders will help you move on to your next opportunity.

Be clear on what you want to do next

When I started working for my manager, he said I would be on the team for only a year. But 12 months became 18 months and then 24 months. He told me to stop worrying and that he would help me find my next opportunity. Four years passed, and he still wouldn't let me go—I had become too valuable to him. And I had made the fatal mistake of tying my career to one individual.

"If your manager isn't supportive of the next step in your career, be vocal with as many leaders as possible in your organization about your career vision," Lola Bakare, owner of consultancy company be/co and marketing executive coach, told me. "Bonus points if you can manage to weave in all the ways in which working with your current manager has inspired you along the way."

She added, "If a number of leaders are advocating for you to move on to your next role, it will be harder for your manager to hold on to you. No one wants to be labeled a talent hoarder, and the public recognition of their role in your success just might turn them into an advocate, too."

Along with following Bakare's advice, connect with HR about your career vision. In many organizations, HR plays a key role in talent planning and will know which roles will be opening up in the short and long terms. People in HR can advocate for you behind closed doors to help you move on to your next opportunity.

Help find your successor

If your manager is convinced that you're the only one who can do your job, it's time to change their mind. Help them find your successor. Consider your own teammates and people you've met in other parts of the organization. Think about who in your networks would be interested in joining your company. Offer to introduce your manager to key talent.

If you have an internal successor in mind, ask them to help you on a project. In this way, you give them the opportunity to see if they like the work and you give your boss the chance to see how talented the person is. And as you plan to move on to your next role internally, help with a smooth transition by supporting your successor. Help prepare them for success by introducing them to key stakeholders and projects and coaching them on how to work with their new manager. Setting your successor up for wins means you won't be pulled into your old role and can move on to your next chapter.

. . .

If you've become so valuable to your manager that your career has stalled, it's time to be dispensable. While you show your value and expertise to your manager and team and make an impact in your current role, set boundaries, take on work you're excited about, network within your organization, and set up the next the person who comes after you for success.

Adapted from content posted on hbr.org, January 10, 2022 (product #H06SQJ).

SECTION THREE

Build Your Support Team

11

Start Building Meaningful Connections

by Jenny Fernandez and Luis Velasquez

The often-repeated observation "It takes a village to raise a child" is popular for a reason. Young people need to interact with and build relationships with a variety of people to grow up well versed and to thrive—and the same advice matters in the workforce and throughout your career.

In the initial stages of your career, one of the most important things you can do is build a village of your own. We're not talking about a college network, LinkedIn friends, or the people who you met one time at a conference. We're referring to the relationships that will have a significant impact on your life over time—ones that can accelerate your path to a promotion, increase your visibility in an organization, and stretch you beyond your comfort zone to become the leader you aspire to be.

Throughout our careers as executive coaches, we've seen success manifest itself through these connections. In fact, there are five relationships that we believe are key to anyone's professional growth. Think of them as your personal board of directors. It will take time to build meaningful relationships with each, so you'd better start now.

The Mentor

When a more experienced person teaches someone new, the knowledge transfer is unparalleled. Some of the most successful people ever have mentors to thank (in part) for their careers. Treasury Secretary Larry Summers mentored Facebook chief operating officer Sheryl Sandberg. Author and poet Maya Angelou mentored Oprah Winfrey, and music legend Ray Charles mentored the equally talented Quincy Jones.

Think of a mentor as the North Star that will keep you on track when you're feeling lost at work. A mentor is the one person you can turn to for guidance inside (or outside) of your organization—whether you are looking to expand your industry knowledge, navigate a difficult conversation, listen to feedback on a project, or get some encouragement when times are tough. This person is reliable, wise, and, most importantly, honest. Mentorship is all about having challenging conversations that help increase your self-awareness and help you grow both personally and professionally.

Great mentors are often proven leaders who have navigated corporate politics and advanced their career in an organization or an industry that aligns with your longer-term goals. To find such a leader, think about someone whose path you deeply admire but who is still within reach, someone who may actually respond to your email or LinkedIn message. A potential mentor has to be open to forming a professional relationship with you because, more often than not, they're pressed for time and mentoring takes effort.

Once you've identified a potential mentor, reach out to them in writing. Don't start with "Would you be my mentor?" These kinds of bonds form slowly after both of you have had a chance to interact and build trust. Instead, share one or two things you admire about their work, and explain why you're contacting them in the first place. You might say, "I attended the digital conference last week and was intrigued by your talk on what makes content go viral. I'm new to this field, and I'm interested in specializing in video production. I'd love to hear your career story and how you got here. Would it be possible for us to have a quick video chat sometime within the next couple of weeks so I can learn more?"

After your initial meeting, take the time to engage with them regularly—potentially quarterly or bimonthly—updating them on your projects, progress, and achievements. These updates will help you develop a reputation as someone who can manage stakeholders and deliver what you set out to do. Building a strong personal brand by displaying your competence, experience, and positive attitude is an effective way to attract the interest of powerful people at your company. Potential mentors will want to advise someone who is already on an upward trajectory.

The Sponsor

While mentors give you advice and perspective, sponsors advocate on your behalf and sometimes directly present you with career advancement opportunities. Sponsors are someone who also works in your company, whereas a mentor may not. They play a role in the "behind closed doors" conversations that you may not be included in, and they can support your boss in advocating for you in front of other members of the leadership team.

Morgan Stanley's managing director Carla Harris gets it right in her TED talk. "A mentor, frankly, is a nice-to-have," she says, "but you can survive a long time in your career without one. You are not going to ascend in any organization without a sponsor."[1]

Research backs her up. A junior manager with a sponsor is 21% more likely to climb up the career ladder than someone in the same position without one.[2] The global think tank and advisory group Coqual even coined the phrase *sponsor effect* to describe the way that high power is transferred in the workplace. Its research found that "one in four white men in the middle ranks of workplaces have sponsorship, but only one in eight women and just one in 20 minorities have them," indicating opportunities for greater sponsorship among women and other underrepresented groups for advancement.

To find a sponsor, you need to begin by showing people in your organization that you're someone worth advocating for. This means you must be great at what you do—and your work must be visible.

Start by thinking about what unique skills, cultural knowledge, or generational life experiences you can share with your organization to add value to its mission and to help it reach outstanding goals. For example, if you work at an agency that is looking to bring innovative advertising offerings to its clients, your manager might be interested in learning more about emerging video-sharing networks like TikTok or live-streaming platforms like Twitch. If you have firsthand experience with these technologies, then offer to host a Zoom "brown bag" lunch to share your knowledge.

Sponsors, like mentors, are in high demand and difficult to recruit. But if you develop a standout reputation, they might end up coming to you. Alternatively, you may be able to ask your mentor to make an introduction or you might reach out yourself for an introductory chat over coffee. Whatever you do, the first time you meet with a potential sponsor, be sure to enter the conversation with a purpose. Ask them questions about their career path, work, passions, and goals. Then share your own. You want to build a foundation of good intention and rapport.

The Partner

A partnership is a mutually beneficial peer relationship. It is fueled by trust, a shared drive to succeed, and the recognition that you can do better together. Your partner is an ally who can serve as a sounding board to broaden your perspective, a collaborator to tackle problems with, and a connector who can help you build out your personal brand and expand your network.

Your partner is not always your work BFF. This relationship is more transactional. You each have an explicit intent to elevate yourselves by elevating each other.

One powerful example of a partnership can be observed through the women in President Barack Obama's administration. They used an *amplification strategy* to support one another and make their collective voices heard: When a woman made a key point during a meeting, the other women would repeat it, giving credit to its author.

Simply put, finding a partner is similar to finding a cofounder—look for someone whose personality and work ethic complement your own. You want a person who will fill the gaps in your working style. For instance, if you are more of an introvert who avoids public speaking, look for a partner who enjoys presenting and will promote your shared projects when doing so. If you are a strategic person who prefers the big picture, look for a partner who is strong in the details of analytics and operations. You should also choose a partner, such as a peer or a cross-functional team member, who is working toward the same outcome that you are pursuing.

As a good first step toward building this relationship, become an advocate for other people's work. Pay attention to who reciprocates your enthusiasm. They may be a good candidate for the role. Ultimately, what makes a partnership work is the idea that you two will be more successful together.

The Competitor

The business world is full of rivalries: Steve Jobs versus Bill Gates. Jeff Bezos versus Elon Musk. Indra Nooyi versus Irene Rosenfeld. Some of these rivalries have resulted in amazing breakthroughs.

Competition can be healthy if it's focused on achieving results (a win-win) rather than on a battle for resources (a win-lose). When used correctly, it can serve as a motivation to hone your skills and can lead to improved performance, breakthrough ideas, and a greater drive to get things done.

Your competitor could be your ally or even your partner. Imagine that you and a peer come up with two great ideas for executing a project. You know that both of you have the potential to think up unique and separately effective solutions. Instead of butting heads and trying to choose one over the other, how might the result look if you collaborated and came up with something that's much more effective and valuable?

That's what competitors can do. The idea is to win, not win over.

Remember that competitive relationships show up naturally at work. As Stephen Covey stresses in his business classic *The 7 Habits of Highly Effective People*, a win-win attitude includes three vital character traits: integrity, maturity, and an abundance mentality. So, choose your competitor after evaluating these traits. Once you have identified a potential competitor in your company, schedule a one-on-one meeting. One way to entice this person to work with you instead of against you is to have a vulnerable conversation. Be sure to tell them you admire them professionally and consider them a formidable peer. Then, share your aspirations, ask them about their goals, and figure out if there are ways you can help each other succeed.

The Mentee

Most of us are familiar with the aphorism, "If you want to master something, teach it." Most of us have been teachers at some point in our lives, whether we're teaching our friends how to play a card game, our kids how to ride a bike, or our classmates how to better understand a difficult concept. No matter the situation, assuming the role of the teacher helps you gain greater clarity of a subject by breaking it down into simple steps or by articulating a complex problem in a more understandable way.

At work, having a mentee serves this purpose—it allows you to be the teacher. Whether you help onboard an intern or assist a new colleague in navigating the specifics of a project they've been assigned, you learn more by teaching more.

Becoming a mentor also helps you improve important soft skills that every leader should have: strong communication, creativity, and empathy. Employers are looking to develop leaders who can provide clear direction, be innovative problem solvers, and who have emotional intelligence. As a mentor, you are a leader and role model. You learn to bring out the best in others, recognize their strengths, give feedback, and coach. Thus, this role will push you to be better and to strive for more.

Seek out mentoring opportunities internally by looking for interns or new employees who may need help settling in. You can also find this role externally by mentoring in affinity organizations such as your alma mater or a nonprofit. That said, if you are a mentor at your workplace, this role will give you more visibility and will help build up that good reputation we've discussed.

Sometimes, these relationships will be formed randomly and without effort. But you can accomplish so much more if you are open and *intentional* about it. So, don't leave things to chance. As a popular saying goes, "Luck is what happens when preparation meets opportunity."

Adapted from "5 Relationships You Need to Build a Successful Career," Ascend, on hbr.org, June 4, 2021.

12

How to Find a Mentor

by Janet T. Phan

In the summer of 2004, I was 18 years old, preparing for my first year of college and looking for ways to fund my education. I was working double shifts at a fast-food restaurant and late nights at a movie theater, and yet, one day, I found myself at a gas station without enough money to fill up my tank.

I promised myself to do whatever it would take to never be in this situation again: one where I was living from paycheck to paycheck, working multiple jobs, and couch surfing to save money on rent. Working harder—in my case, 12-hour days—wasn't getting me anywhere, but I knew that working smarter could. As the child of refugee parents from Vietnam, I didn't have anyone at home who understood how to navigate the American school system or workforce. I knew I needed help, someone to guide me.

A good mentor can make a huge imprint on your life. And thanks to not one but many mentors, I was able to grow from that woman stuck at the gas station into who

I am now. I turned to my former high school teacher, a person I could trust, who advocated for my education and gave me advice that prepared me to succeed in college. A few years after I graduated, I started an IT internship where I met a mentor who helped jumpstart my career in technology. Today, I'm a senior technical product manager working to launch satellites that provide affordable and reliable broadband to underserved and underrepresented communities around the world. I'm also the founder of Thriving Elements, a global nonprofit mentoring program for underserved, underrepresented girls.

My work has taught me some valuable lessons, but perhaps the most important is that no matter what stage you're at, it's worth learning how to make an ask, nurture, and maintain these kinds of relationships. Fostered correctly, mentors can put you in the driver's seat of your career, empower you to explore options that were previously unimaginable, give you access to untapped opportunities, and teach you how to navigate the challenges you never saw coming.

Here are a few tips on how you can find mentors and nurture and maintain those relationships.

Asking for That First Meeting

Seventy-six percent of people say that mentors are important, but only thirty-seven percent actually have one. Why the gap? In my experience, people lack mentors because most of us are afraid to ask for that initial meeting. The fear of rejection is real. Reaching out to someone you admire but who you may not know so well—especially if that person is more senior than you—is intimidating.

To take some pressure off yourself and ease the fear, remind yourself that the people you admire have likely had various mentors throughout their lives. This person probably had someone who helped them to get to where they are today, and they would jump at the opportunity to help others in the same way. If you want to connect with them, start with a simple request: a quick 15- to 30-minute virtual coffee break.

The best way to reach out is usually sending a short email. Share one or two things you admire about their work, then tell them a little about yourself, why you're reaching out, and what you would like to learn from them. Then wrap it up with your request:

> *Dear X,*
>
> *I've been reading about the work you're doing with Y. I'm interested in building my career in technology, and I'd love to hear how you rose from a systems analyst to a technical product manager in five years. Would it be possible for us to have a quick video chat sometime within the next couple of weeks?*

A first meeting over coffee or a short video call is low commitment for your target mentor and will give you an opportunity to better understand them, gauge your chemistry (more on chemistry in chapter 13), and see if they'd be the right fit for you.

Nurturing the Relationship

The number one recommendation I've heard from both the mentors and the mentees I've worked with over the years is this: Take the time to really connect with the other person.

Get to know them

Think of your first coffee meeting or virtual call as an opportunity for casual conversation. Remember that you're both still feeling each other out, so don't just focus the discussion on work. Ask your potential mentor what they like to do on the weekends, what books they like to read, or what hobbies they're interested in. Most people will be thrilled to take a break from their hectic workdays and connect on a personal level. This kind of conversation also gives both of you a chance to see if you have anything in common and whether you enjoy one another's company.

Toward the middle of the first meeting, it's appropriate to bring up career questions you have for them and to talk about the areas in which you'd like to grow. As you wrap up the call, summarize the advice they've provided to show that you value their input. For instance, you might say, "It sounds like attending networking events really helped you advance your career. I'll look into some virtual meetups that I can use to connect with other people in my field. Thanks for that suggestion."

Send a thank-you note

After your meeting, follow up with a thank-you email sometime within the same week. In your message, share a few key things you learned during the conversation, and let the person know you'd like to follow up in a few weeks:

> *Hi X,*
>
> *I loved learning about your hike in Vietnam and all the wonderful food you tried along the way. I think I might go to the Vietnamese restaurant nearby and give the cuisine a try. I was also surprised to hear that you taught yourself how to code through online courses. That is so inspiring! If it's okay with you, I'll touch base in a few weeks.*

Most people in a position to mentor are busy, so don't be alarmed if it takes them a few days to respond.

Follow up

Three to five weeks after sending the thank-you message, follow up to let your potential mentor know what you did in light of your discussions in that first meeting. (Did you read the book they recommended or watch a TED talk they seemed to have loved?) Then, ask if they would be willing to meet up again in the next couple of weeks. I don't recommend sending an agenda. Rather, try to keep your tone and suggestions casual. In my experience, good leaders and mentors appreciate a more informal setting. The point is to create an atmosphere that's enjoyable for both of you—not schedule yet another work meeting. That said, it can be helpful to jot down things you'd like to discuss and share them in your email when reaching out:

> *Hi X,*
>
> *I finally got down to reading that book, and I have to say, I can't believe I didn't read it sooner. What a great story of grit and determination. Thank you for recommending it.*
>
> *I was planning to take a course in creative writing from Y institute. Are you familiar with it? Maybe we can discuss during our next catch-up? I know you're very busy, but let me know if you'd have time to meet up in the next couple of weeks. I'd really appreciate it.*

Embrace the Awkwardness of the Ask

BY MARK HOROSZOWSKI

Asking someone to be your mentor the first time, the second time, and even the third time is a little awkward. You've probably never been asked to mentor someone else or learned how to ask someone to be a mentor to you. Embrace the uncomfortable feeling, and allow yourself to be vulnerable. There is no harm that can come from asking, but take it slow. Ask someone for a first conversation to learn more about their work and interests. Once you learn more about each other, if there is an alignment, then make the bigger request for mentorship. Asking someone cold to be a mentor with a long email is too much for that person to take in.

When you feel ready, make a clear request: "I've really enjoyed this conversation. Would it be okay if I followed up with you again in one month after I make some progress toward my goals?"

If the person confirms they will meet with you again, send an email proposing an agenda and hinting at the idea of a longer-term relationship. Something like "In our next chat, I hope we have a quick catch-up, and then I'd love to further expand on our conversation from last time. I'll come prepared with some specific questions that I think you could help me answer."

Adapted from "How to Build a Great Relationship with a Mentor," on hbr.org, January 21, 2020 (product #H05D1E).

Usually after three or four meetings, you'll have a good sense of whether you'd like the person to be your mentor, at which point you can say something like, "These meetings have been very helpful to me; it's almost like you're my mentor!" Then pause and see their reaction.

If they reciprocate with a yes, that's good news for you. If they smile but don't respond directly, that's okay too. It's likely because they don't want to formally commit to mentorship right now. But don't be discouraged. As long as they're making time to meet with you and you're getting the guidance you need, there's really no need for a label.

Maintaining the Relationship

When you ask someone to be your mentor, you are also asking them to invest their time in you. Show them that their time is being well used by demonstrating a return on their investment.

Keep them updated

As a mentor myself, I can say there's nothing more rewarding than seeing that the time I've invested in a mentee was valuable and helped them advance toward their goals. But it's a mentee's job to help the mentor see just how they've done so. Remember the first follow-up email you sent? Make that a regular thing. Use the time between your catch-ups to take action on the goals you set with your mentor. Send them updates (a simple text or an email) telling them how their guidance is playing an important role in your career and personal development. But be sure not to spam them. About once every month or two is good during the first year, and as time progresses and you've established a good mentoring relationship, pinging your mentor even once a quarter is okay. The goal is to keep in touch and to keep them informed about how your career is progressing.

Offer to help

Like any other relationship, the mentoring relationship is a two-way street. What you're giving back to your mentor is really your progress, but there's also no harm in checking in with your mentor during your meetings to see if you can help them in any way. Maybe they're working on a presentation and could use an outside perspective, or perhaps you know someone they were looking to connect with.

Express gratitude

Write a thank-you note after each meeting. While it doesn't need to be as extensive as your first note, a quick "Thanks again for your time, was great to catch up!" will show them that you appreciate the time and guidance they are giving to you.

. . .

Mentorship can be life-changing. I'm proof of that. Staying in the driver's seat and being proactive will make your relationship with your mentor a successful one. Use these principles to guide you toward a future you've imagined for yourself.

Adapted from "What's the Right Way to Find a Mentor?," Ascend, on hbr.org, March 10, 2021.

13

Build Chemistry with Your Mentor

by Janice Omadeke

There's plenty of advice out there about the value of mentorship and the steps you can take to find a mentor. But what is less talked about is the intangible ingredient that transforms any relationship from functional to rewarding. That's chemistry.

A lot of people put chemistry in a silo with romantic relationships, but the word itself has a few meanings. In this context, I want to focus on a singular definition: chemistry as "an interaction between people working together," more specifically, an interaction that is "harmonious or effective." This kind of connection often takes place when two people are drawn, or attracted, to one another, and it can—and often does—manifest itself in completely platonic or professional relationships.

Think of two magnets that, because of their material makeup, are pulled together by a field of magnetic energy completely invisible to our eyes. The word *chemistry* can be used to describe a similar, nonromantic attraction between two people: friends you immediately click with, professors who always seem to get your work, and colleagues or business partners who you could brainstorm with for hours. You probably have strong chemistry with these people.

Just like any other great relationship, a mentorship needs chemistry to reach its full potential, for a few reasons:

- People who feel naturally connected to one another have an easier time building a foundation of trust, and trust opens the door to honest conversation.
- When there's positive energy between two people, it's often accompanied by an eagerness to learn more from each other, ask questions, and share knowledge.
- Both people feel committed and valued because they genuinely enjoy one another's company—the mentorship feels less transactional and is less likely to lead to burnout.
- There's a mutual investment in one another's success, meaning the mentorship will last longer and produce better results.

In short, if you and your mentor don't naturally enjoy each other, you are going to be less emotionally invested and your relationship will probably fall a little flat.

Identifying Chemistry

Luckily, unlike magnets, the chemistry between two people is *not always* instantaneous, and it can even develop over time. So if it's not already obvious, how do you know that there is chemistry, present or potential, between you and your mentor? The following questions can help you figure it out.

Comfort

- Do you feel comfortable opening up to this person?
- Can you share your goals, your ideas, and your fears?
- Do you trust this person to listen to you with an open mind and offer advice based on experience and empathy—not on judgment?
- Do they believe in you and want you to succeed?

If you know or sense that the answer to any of these questions is no, then you and your (potential) mentor probably lack good chemistry right now.

Connection

- Do you feel a basic connection with this person?
- Do you genuinely care for them? For instance, do you feel happy when they succeed and empathy when they are going through challenges?
- Removed from the professional environment, would you be okay grabbing lunch with this person, going on a hike together, or doing some similar joint activity?
- When you interact, are there frequent awkward pauses, or does the conversation flow naturally?

While it's normal to have conversation flow better on some days than others, if keeping the discussion going feels like pulling teeth, then the chemistry is probably lacking. Similarly, if you find it hard to empathize with this person or vice versa, then it's likely that neither of you feels a comfortable connection.

Click or Clash

- Do you look forward to your meetings with this person?
- Does the person seem equally interested in meeting with you?
- Do you feel energized in each other's presence?

If you both look forward to seeing each other, that's a sign of strong chemistry. If you dread the meeting and secretly hope that one of you will cancel last minute, it's time to admit that things probably aren't going to work.

When the Chemistry Isn't Exactly There

You now have a better idea of where you and your (potential) mentor stand. If you feel good about your relationship, congratulations! Great chemistry is not easy to come by. If you found yourself disappointed by your answers to the preceding questions, what can you do to build chemistry with someone you admire?

Transparency about your intentions, including where you want the relationship to go, is a good way to strengthen your connection with someone and set the foundation for chemistry to develop. Clearly explain your professional goals and the role you hope the other person can play in helping you reach them. Through this conversation, you can quickly determine whether there is potential for you and the other person to align.

For instance, you might say, "I was really hoping to develop my leadership skills this year [or another goal you are trying to reach]. I know you have a lot of experience in this area, and I'd love your input on a few things I'm struggling with." Follow up with any questions you may have, and listen to their feedback. Perhaps this person can help you with something that they hadn't realized they could do, or maybe you and this person can continue working together to build goals separately now that everything is on the table.

At the same time, if you find that their advice is just not resonating or feels inauthentic, then it may be time to throw in the towel. In this case, try not to feel discouraged. You're not going to find chemistry with every person, but if you are intentional with the relationships you pursue, it is possible.

Finding Chemistry

What if you're starting from scratch? How do you up your chances of finding chemistry with a potential mentor?

Historically, many companies have taken a traditional approach to mentorship—pairing people who look like one another and who self-identify as being similar to one another. There is nothing inherently wrong with this approach. We all want to be validated, to see ourselves reflected in others in the world, and to know that we are not alone. A mentor who shares your experiences can be incredibly valuable in helping you navigate your work (and life), and seeking this kind of relationship can certainly increase your likelihood of finding chemistry.

Even so, focusing exclusively on connecting with people who are just like you can also be problematic, as it can result in groupthink and make it difficult for people from different communities or backgrounds to connect with and learn from one another. That's why you can—and you should—also try to build mentorships and find chemistry with people who are different from yourself, especially if you want to broaden your viewpoints and strengthen your network.

With that in mind, let's focus on a couple of alternative approaches to mentorship—ones that expand on the more traditional model and are focused on creating inclusive work environments by helping people across generations and life experiences to collaborate and connect.

Peer-to-Peer Mentoring

This approach to mentorship involves creating lateral connections with people who are at the same level, or close to the same level, that you are at work. Peer-to-peer mentoring removes generational gulfs and allows people of varying ages and backgrounds to connect through the commonalities of their jobs. Both participants can be open and can grow and learn, knowing that the power dynamic is equal, and no one holds seniority over the other. Because the mentorship begins with a strong foundation of shared experience and perspective, there is a real chance for chemistry to arise.

Group Mentoring

For some, the group mentorship model might be preferable. With this approach, one or more mentors typically work with a group of mentees. Although group mentoring may not be as intimate as other models, it allows mentees *and mentors* to easily connect with a larger number of people, upping the chances of finding real connections.

. . .

Chemistry may, to some extent, be out of our control—but it can be found in a professional setting. When you do find chemistry in your connections, you will see your mentorships—or any kind of working relationship, for that matter—flourish. Who knows? Chemistry may even develop when you least expect it.

Adapted from "The Secret to a Great Mentorship? Chemistry," Ascend, on hbr.org, January 21, 2022.

14

Network with People Outside Your Industry

by Dorie Clark

Most professionals build their network over time through proximity—people from your business school study group or colleagues from your current company or past jobs. You may have a few outliers in the mix, but unless you've been deliberate about your networking, the vast majority of people you know probably work in the same field or industry as yours. Your more limited circle of connections may seem innocuous, but this inadvertent myopia can put you at serious professional risk.

First, if your network has become too narrow, you limit your options in case of a career change or a downturn in your company or industry. If coworkers are the only people you know well and you find yourself in the midst of layoffs, there's no one to turn to for outside assistance.

Additionally, you're more prone to fall into groupthink if you're not exposed to diverse points of view. As Harvard sociologist Robert Putnam has asserted, you need to have a balance of both "bonding capital" and "bridging capital." That is, you need relationships based on your commonalities (bonding) and relationships built across differences (bridging). Relationships with people similar to you may feel more natural, but it pays to push beyond your comfort zone. Indeed, research shows that companies with more diverse boards enjoy better financial performance.

Dan, a senior professional I interviewed for my first book, *Reinventing You*, realized that he hadn't invested enough in his own bridging capital. He had spent a decade at a large technology company, rising to become an engineering director. But it occurred to him that his entire professional network consisted of people from that company. Given the vagaries of industry disruption, he became concerned.

He embarked on a networking campaign that forced him to meet once a week with people outside the company: executive recruiters, venture capitalists, startup entrepreneurs, and more. His connections allowed him to move to an exciting new job and immediately prove his value, thanks to the industry insights he'd gained from meeting with so many people.

To diversify your own network, here are four strategies you can follow.

Inventory your existing connections

First, take an inventory of your current network. Who are the five to 10 people you spend the most time with? Next, make a list of your *outer circle*—the 50 or so people who matter the most in your professional life. Do a quick scan to evaluate the professional diversity of your network, noting whether your connections are inside or outside your company and whether they share your profession. If your network is weighted more than 70% in any direction (for example, if 85% of your closest contacts are fellow marketers), it's time to think hard about how to diversify. Identify past colleagues or friends whom you enjoy and who are in different fields or at different companies but whom you haven't spent much time with. Take this as your cue to reach out and propose getting together; they'll often welcome the invitation.

Put networking on your schedule

Part of Dan's success in broadening his network outside his company was his decision to make networking a deliberate part of his weekly routine. As an introvert, he'd previously eschewed most networking events. But when he realized his circle had become dangerously small, he committed to regular breakfast meetings with new colleagues. Networking is never urgent and will often be the first activity jettisoned when things get busy at work, but it's essential to prioritize it by putting it on your schedule.

Ask for recommendations

Almost everyone's network is disproportionately composed of people like themselves. So take advantage of this fact, and make your network stand out. If you're looking to diversify your professional relationships, ask the people who are outliers in your network to recommend people they think you should meet. You could say to them, "I'd like to know more angel investors, and you're really plugged into those circles—who else do you think I should connect with? Would you be willing to make an introduction?"

Don't look for immediate returns

Some people end up with a narrow network because of inertia, but others don't extend themselves, because they just don't see the potential for return. If you work in finance, making friends with a filmmaker is obviously less likely to add to your bottom line than is spending time with someone in your own industry. But you have to play the long game. People—including you—may change careers, and that far-reaching connection may prove helpful down the line. Additionally, you can't predict who will be in someone else's network; the filmmaker may have gone to high school with a CEO you'd now like to do business with.

The best reason to build a professionally diverse network, however, isn't about what you'll get out of those relationships. It's to fulfill personal curiosity and develop yourself as a person; professional or monetary return on investment is a happy coincidence. For several years, I've been hosting dinner gatherings of eight to 10 interesting people from a mix of professions. It didn't seem relevant that one of my friends was a comedian and another a comedy promoter, until I started doing stand-up performances and was able to access helpful advice that saved me time and frustration.

. . .

It's easy to coast through life only connecting with people like ourselves. But by expending the extra effort to increase our bridging capital, we're gaining access to new insights and creating more "career insurance" for ourselves by broadening the ranks of people who know, like, and respect our work.

Adapted from "Start Networking with People Outside Your Industry," on hbr.org, October 20, 2016 (product #H0377W).

SECTION FOUR

Embrace Change and Uncertainty

15

Take Time Off Between Jobs

by Rebecca Zucker

Changing jobs is an ideal opportunity to take time off, and we all know that having sufficient downtime is instrumental in starting any new job refreshed and recharged, ready to take on a new challenge. In an ideal world, we would take sabbaticals in between jobs; such a break can be particularly helpful in the case of burnout. A sabbatical is not focused job-search time but is mostly downtime devoted to creative and personal pursuits (which may include some career exploration) and can last anywhere from a month to a year.

I took a yearlong sabbatical in Paris earlier in my career after working a few years in investment banking and then in an equally demanding job in strategic planning. This extended time off allowed me to reevaluate and reset the course of my career and life for the better. But the break was not something I could have negotiated with any prospective employer, given the duration. Some sectors, such as banking, mandate garden leave (typically a few months long) for certain employees in between jobs as a noncompete provision, where the departing employee is still paid. However, few people have the luxury of this type of leave or other extended sabbaticals.

In most cases, when you find a new job, either you have already left your prior employer (and are unemployed) or you are still working. If you are unemployed, your time off has probably been riddled with uncertainty and anxiety. This period can deplete your energy and feels very little like a rejuvenating vacation. And if you find a new job while fully employed, whether you were actively seeking a new role or unexpectedly presented with an exciting opportunity, it can feel like going from the frying pan into the fire if you don't have sufficient time off before starting your new job.

The question, then, for many people when changing jobs is often, "Can I negotiate time off before I start my new job, and how much is reasonable to ask for?"

First, you can (and should) absolutely negotiate time off before you start. Research shows that negotiations are more successful when they are multi-issue negotiations, and your start date is one of many variables up for discussion. As with any negotiation, you need to have a good sense of what's most important to you (and the other party) and where you are willing to give in one area to receive more in another.

If you already feel rested and are ready to get started, then you may need less time off. Over the years, I've counseled many clients who are eager and prepared to dive into their new position. I've told them that taking a shorter break can provide tremendous leverage in obtaining something else that's more important to them—such as higher compensation that will pay off for years to come. In my experience coaching hundreds of clients over two decades on job negotiations, a hiring manager will often gladly pay more if that is what will clinch the deal for you to start ASAP and start making their life easier that much sooner.

However, if you are looking to take a real break before plunging into your new job, here are several factors to consider in determining how much time to request:

Business Needs

Keep in mind that the organization is hiring you because they have a clear and present need. According to Sally Thornton, CEO and founder of Forshay, an executive recruiting and on-demand consulting firm, "It absolutely needs to start with the business needs. You don't want to take a job where they're preparing to go IPO and you're like, 'Hey, I need six weeks.' If the company has a specific milestone, it's [about] being really thoughtful to that milestone that they have to deal with."

If the company more generally has a lot of work to do, and they just want you to be there as soon as possible, Thornton advises taking at least two weeks off between jobs to "take a breath."

Appropriate Notice

Another consideration if you are going to a new job directly from a current employer is the importance of giving ample notice and smoothly handing off projects to your colleagues. You want to make sure to end well, preserving both the goodwill and the relationships you've built. In the United States, the standard minimum notice is typically two weeks. You may contractually be bound to more. Add this to the actual time off you'd like to take, and it can easily be a month before you start your new job.

Further, many people prefer to err on the side of caution and avoid giving formal notice to their current employer until their background check has cleared. These checks can take anywhere from a few days to a few weeks. Lourdes Olvera-Marshall, a diversity and inclusion professional and an executive coach who has negotiated start dates at three new jobs over the last dozen years, advised, "Don't commit to a specific start date before your background check goes through and the offer is official. You can give a timeframe instead and phrase it as 'Once the offer is official, I will give two to three weeks' notice and then will need two weeks before starting. If there's a specific need on the start date, we can chat about it.'" Speak in terms of number of weeks versus a calendar date. Otherwise, if the background check takes longer than anticipated, it will eat into your time off.

Financial Considerations

Personal or family financial needs are also relevant in determining how much time you take off before starting your new job. Will you still have health-care coverage from your prior employer, or will you need to sign up for COBRA? Typically, in the United States, if you work through the first of the month, you'll have health-care coverage for that whole month. If you've been unemployed for an extended period, need health care, or have material financial obligations like school tuition or a mortgage, a few weeks' additional salary from a new job may mean a lot less stress for you.

Moreover, if it's near the end of the year, you'll probably want to stay at your current employer until you receive your bonus or vesting of equity, unless your new employer is willing to make up the financial difference for leaving beforehand. Likewise, you'll want to ask your new employer about when you will be eligible for a bonus, retirement benefits, company matching, and new health benefits. These effective dates may provide a significant financial incentive to start earlier—in Olvera-Marshall's case, it was only the difference of a few days. Fortunately, she made a point to ask the recruiter, "What benefits are affected by my start date?"

Personal Needs

You may also need time off to take care of important things you've been putting off. For example, you might want to visit family (a visit might warrant a few weeks if they're in another country), have an elective surgery, or do home repairs you've been delaying. If your new job requires a significant move, such as cross-country or even overseas, you will need some time—particularly if you have to sell your home (or at least get it ready to put it on the market). Ask for the time you need for these types of priorities.

When one client's daughter was getting married, the client asked for a start date after the wedding, which was in a few weeks. In this way, she could not only enjoy the final planning stages but also avoid having to handle last-minute wedding details during her first week of a big, new job. You might say, for example, "I need some time to take care of some family obligations. I'd rather take the time for this before joining the company so that I won't have any distractions and can be fully focused on my new job once I start."

Time to Decompress

Perhaps most important is having sufficient time to relax and recharge so that you are ready to start your new job refreshed and energized. Research published in the *Journal of Happiness Studies* shows that the ideal vacation length is eight days. Caroline Stokes, CEO of FORWARD, an executive search, says, "I usually suggest to the people I place that they take a few weeks off to transition their brain by taking time away—ideally a trip away, which has been more challenging during Covid, but to at least get away to create some distance and recharge their brain for a new challenge."

Your new employer might say, "We really need you right now." Barring any specific, time-sensitive business imperative, don't be afraid to ask for time to take a real break. This opportunity may not come again for several years. You can say, "I understand there's a lot of work to be done. I may not have this opportunity again for some time, and I will be much more clearheaded, creative, and productive if I can fully decompress before diving in and giving this job my all." James, a client of mine, reflected on a prior transition where he finished one job on a Friday and started his next job on the following Monday. He said, "It was stressful and made me feel resentful. . . . I do think that it may have made me seem less open, friendly, and eager than I would have otherwise, so it was a missed opportunity to make the best possible first impression."

Time to Ramp Up

You may also want to budget some time before you start to ramp up. During this period, you might, for example, read any relevant documents (strategic plans, customer surveys, etc.) or schedule meetings for your first week with your boss, key stakeholders, and direct reports (since calendars can fill up weeks in advance). You might also use this time to confirm the details of your introduction to the team or company and to complete HR paperwork ahead of your start date so that you can dive right into your new responsibilities.

Overall, the consensus is that one month is the peak of the bell curve in terms of how much time to request. Thornton noted, "I've never seen anyone take more than a month when it's an active job." There may be occasions where you can request more time. If you can't get the break you want, it may be an opportunity to negotiate more time off later.

The important thing is to ask for what you need and to have an open conversation about the trade-offs. "If it's not a clear conversation about trade-offs and how it impacts your life, then you're not actually having a full conversation," Thornton said. What's more, this discussion—like any other negotiation—will be indicative of your relationship going forward with the company. Is it open, understanding, and collaborative, or based on fear and lacking compromise? In the grand scheme of things, a month (or even a bit more) isn't all that much.

Adapted from "How Much Time Can I Take Off Between Jobs?," on hbr.org, October 27, 2021 (product #H06NRU).

16

When You Need Time Off for Health Reasons

A conversation with Laurie Edwards

There is little guidance out there for communicating a health crisis or chronic illness to your bosses and coworkers. Our private health—what's happening inside our minds and bodies—is often still invisible to colleagues. When an acute or a chronic health issue disrupts our work life, how do we let our bosses and coworkers know? How vulnerable should we be?

Women at Work cohosts Amy Bernstein and Emily Caulfield posed these questions to Laurie Edwards, a writer, a teaching professor at Northeastern University, and an advocate for people with chronic illnesses. Edwards has had to consider these questions while navigating as a writer with multiple chronic illnesses, including a rare genetic lung disease, and she shares advice on disclosing and discussing health issues with colleagues.

AMY BERNSTEIN: Earlier in the episode, our colleague Maureen shared that when she was managing a health issue and learning how to disclose it to her colleagues, she felt uncertain, in denial, and nervous about distressing people. Among all the fears and uncertainties that Maureen shared, was there one that you related to particularly, and that you feel you've made peace with, or figured out for yourself?

LAURIE EDWARDS: The point that really jumped out at me was the idea of [her] not wanting to share information or disclose because she was fearful that maybe people would think that she wasn't competent or wasn't going to be able to do the work. Or that she was somehow not being there for her team, or that whole idea of, "Will you think of me the same way if you know this about me?" And that's absolutely something that I can relate to. It's an ongoing struggle when you live with chronic illness. These days I handle it with more grace and experience but it's definitely still a challenge. I think it really speaks to the nature of either invisible or chronic and serious illness. Because those illnesses and those symptoms will wax and wane and flare and then get a little better, and they're so unpredictable that it's this ongoing tension.

AMY: What advice could you share with our listeners who are dealing with that same kind of fear and anxiety? Anything you've picked up along the way that helps you cope?

LAURIE: The big question is, when do you disclose illness, right? For me, the rule of thumb has always been—and it's information I got from a wonderful longtime collaborator, Rosalind Joffe, who's written about work and chronic illness quite a bit—is when you're no longer able to do the job as it stands, then it's time to have a conversation.

EMILY CAULFIELD: Laurie, as someone who's dealt with chronic illnesses and who's worked with other people with chronic illnesses, what advice would you give someone who has to tell their manager or tell their direct reports about a chronic illness or about a health issue at work?

LAURIE: That's probably one of the most difficult decisions, and I will offer the caveat that of course there's no one-size-fits-all answer. It will depend on the patient, the symptoms, the relationships. The big overarching rule that I follow and recommend is, when you're not able to do the job as it stands, then you have that conversation. And when you have that conversation, you have to be clear and specific about what your needs are. If there's someone that you work with who doesn't necessarily need all the details, but what they really need to help *you* be the best employee is to know, how is this illness specifically impacting this aspect of a job, and what is the plan? What is the potential proposal for addressing that?

EMILY: Right. So, there's no obligation to share the specifics of the illness if you don't feel comfortable doing that.

LAURIE: No, I really encourage people to think in very concrete, actionable, and specific terms of "What is the job? What is the obstacle to me as the employee doing the job as it stands and doing it well, the way I would want to?" And then, "What are the specific things we can discuss to try to alleviate that?"

AMY: I'm wondering if you have any counsel to offer managers who want to be supportive when their folks come to them and disclose that they're dealing with a medical issue.

LAURIE: Absolutely. I've had this interesting experience in my own career where, for periods of time, I have been in a manager position, and so, I've been on the other side of that question. My own experiences have really helped me respond to both students who might be coming to me or when I have overseen instructors in my job who have personal health problems. The conversation flips to: "How can I support you?" Or hopefully, that's the ideal: to respond from a point of view: . . . "What do you need in order to continue to do what you're doing?" Often the accommodations or requests are fairly simple. That's not always the case, of course, but a little bit of flexibility and a little bit of collaboration can make a big difference.

Amy, I know you have a lot of experience as a supervisor in a more management role. In my experience, as an employee, I really needed flexibility with course scheduling. There are certain times of day where it's hard for me to be on campus because I need to fit in physical therapy five days a week for my lung condition. The ability to not have courses very early or very late, or to teach some of them online, has been a huge life-changing accommodation. I've been able to have a conversation with my employer and to say, "These are my scheduling needs. Let's talk about it. What can we do?" I've been very lucky and fortunate that I've been able to work those things out. It's not always that easy, and the needs aren't always that low-hanging fruit. But what kinds of advice would you offer as someone with a lot of management experience for how those conversations could go, or what would you say to employees who are approaching you with potential problems and needs?

AMY: Let me start with the first question, which is that I really do think that you have to respect the individual's need for privacy, and gauging that is sort of one of the first things I try to do. And it's not a direct question: "How much privacy do you want?" It's more of listening to the words they've used and looking at their body language. I mean, of course, the first reaction is, I just want to hug people who are in a situation that frightens them. Or where they feel imperiled. But then, from my perspective, [it's about] trying to think together about a path forward to make the next six weeks or six months viable and comfortable for the person.

LAURIE: I really appreciate what you are saying about what can we do to work together because I think from my own perspective being in that vulnerable position myself, feeling like your employer is invested in working with and not against me, makes such a big difference and can really ease some of that anxiety, and that fear. Because it's really hard to be vulnerable, even if you're disclosing the absolute minimum amount of medical information. It's a hard place to be.

AMY: So, I want to bring in a question from one of our listeners. She's going to need to take six weeks or more off from work to deal with a health condition that she describes as sensitive. And she's worried that when she comes back, she's going to be judged as weak and incompetent by her manager and she'll be denied future promotions and other opportunities. Any thoughts for her to help her through this?

LAURIE: That is such a real and understandable and human fear. At the end of the day whether you have been sick with things your whole life; whether you have some sort of acute, temporary health condition that you need to recover from, and there is a finite recovery period; or whether you have something chronic. People get sick. Things happen. And I think that it's easy to say that from the outside and much harder when you're the one with that health problem and the fear and the anxiety about it. If we can try to extend to ourselves a little bit of understanding and from the outside, if it were happening to somebody else, our reaction would most likely be of concern and wanting to be supportive. And not everyone is going to be in an environment where that's the reaction they get. But I think if we can just focus on what we do know and what we can control and make a plan, and be very communicative, "Here's how long I'm going to be out. Here's how I'm going to delegate the work." I think that hopefully the stigma won't be as present. But realize that it might feel a certain way in those moments of fear and vulnerability.

EMILY: So, Laurie you have a busy work life. You're writing, you're teaching, you're an advocate, and your daughter is also doing remote school from home right now. How have the challenges of managing your illness changed the way that you're managing your career in this moment?

LAURIE: I have had to, in a way that is very uncomfortable for me, work on setting boundaries. I have said no to opportunities that I normally would want to say yes to. I think we're all doing that, whether we have chronic illness or not. I have had to make some tough choices. I have had to sort of say, "Today, this is going to be my best," and give myself more slack than I'm ever used to giving. I think that it's easier for a lot of us and for myself . . . to give other people that [compassionate] side than it is to do that for ourselves. And I think for me, I have 40 years of trying to negotiate a whole "I'm not going to let illness define me or stop me from doing what I want to do" mentality that I continue to negotiate. But yeah, I think at the same time that women have had a crushing impact from the pandemic on our work and in the workforce. A silver lining that I hope can come out of all of this is that employers can see the possibilities of flexibility. And I think that for women with chronic illness and serious illness, that is going to be even more important, just this notion that work doesn't have to look the way you always assume it should for us to be productive and viable members of the workforce.

Adapted from "When You Need Time Off for Health Reasons," Women at Work *podcast season 6, episode 10, December 7, 2020.*

17

Returning to the Workforce After Being a Caregiver

by Rebecca Zucker

Reentering the paid workforce from a full-time caregiving role can feel daunting. Sadly, research has shown that there has historically been a bias against caregiving in recruiting for women, as well as against caregivers who are men, since their caregiving violates gender norms.[1] Regardless of gender, even a short time out of the paid workforce can leave you feeling unsure of yourself—it's like trying to merge onto a fast-moving, busy freeway when you haven't driven for a while.

Here are six strategies to make your reentry less intimidating.

Show yourself some compassion

Even if it's a candidate's market, any job search can be challenging and invariably has its ups and downs. Taking time out of your career for caregiving is a selfless act. As Kristin Neff advises in her book *Self-Compassion: The Proven Power of Being Kind to Yourself*, recognize your common humanity in having to deal with taking care of a loved one. Others will likely show you compassion as well. When my father was dying, I had to pause my client engagements. I was blown away and touched by how understanding my clients were. Since I work mostly with C-level and other senior leaders, many of them had also needed to care for an ailing parent at some point, so they were very understanding of my situation.

Sally Thornton, CEO and founder of Forshay, an executive recruiting and on-demand consulting firm, shared that she is seeing more disclosure in interviews, as early as in the first interview. "Disclosing more about your full life and when you've had to make trade-offs and why you might not have been working is no longer viewed as not being dedicated or ambitious," she said, noting that a bias against caregiving was more prevalent pre-pandemic.

Wanda Cole-Frieman, senior vice president of talent acquisition at CommonSpirit Health, the largest faith-based health system in the United States, concurred. "If there ever was a time in our attitudes around work and people taking time out," she said, "I think this is the time of all times to be able to say, 'Hey, I had to take care of kids. I had to take care of elders. I had to take care of myself,' without there being any stigma." She added, "We are coaching our team [of 150 recruiters] to be empathetic. And we've been in the trenches. We understand what it's like. In the past, I think there were a lot of people who would take time out, where it was this strategic thing: 'When do I tell you? Do I wait until I get the interview?' I just don't see that being such a barrier anymore."

Be transparent

The first thing a recruiter or hiring manager will see is your résumé or LinkedIn profile. Make sure these are up-to-date and that your dates of employment are accurate. You don't want to say that you're still working someplace when you are not or stretch the truth in any way. "A lot of people I see are writing in italics, 'Time out for caregiving,'" Cole-Frieman said. "It's on their résumés or discussed when they're having those initial conversations with their recruiter." She added that she and her team would welcome this disclosure. She also said that if someone prefers to leave a caregiving break off their résumé, it's important to have the dates of employment be accurate. In this case, she said, "it's appropriate to bring [it] up in the first interview. You're saying you want to be back in the workforce; you took some time out. I think it's totally fine."

Share what you've learned

Make it clear that this was time *out*—not time *off*. You probably were just as busy and faced as many challenges. Share what you learned during this time. You might even discuss how you felt about this change, reflecting on how your decision to step back from paid work was either difficult or easy for you. There is power in both reactions to your time away from paid work. The time you spent caregiving shows you can put others' needs before your own; selflessness is a quality of a good team member. Perhaps you had to make high-stakes decisions, weighing short-term and long-term consequences that would affect others' lives or that even had life-and-death implications. Decisions like these have a lot more at stake than does a product launch or a website redesign.

You can also elaborate on the range and complexity of the responsibilities you managed; these skills may have relevance for a job you are seeking. For example, on your résumé and in interviews, you might note that you coordinated your child(ren)'s academic, sports, and social schedules; booked regular medical appointments; aligned end-of-life decisions among three siblings for a parent; oversaw hospice care; served as financial custodian; and settled estate matters. Discuss what was involved and how it ties into the role for which you're applying, if applicable. Cole-Frieman described what she asks candidates who have recently left a caregiving role: "I always want to know, 'Now that you've had some time out, what did you learn, and how would you apply this to your strategic goals in what you have to do and deliver? And what would be different now?' Really thinking about 'How would you use that knowledge and that learning to bring it forth to a new organization, and how would you apply it?' I think that's really key."

Don't dwell on the gap, and don't apologize

While there's much you can share about what you've learned during your time out of the workforce, don't dwell on the gap in employment, and don't apologize for prioritizing your family. Cole-Frieman advised, "I don't think you need to dwell on it. I think be matter-of-fact about it. It shows a lot of who you are and the character that you bring to an organization as well. So I think there are positive things, also, from taking time out. . . . If you're authentic about it and it's real for you, I think that's going to come through."

Further, you still have years of work experience to draw on. Don't lose sight of that. If you find that the recruiter or hiring manager is too focused on when you were out of the workforce than when you were in the workforce, tactfully shift their attention to your earlier work experience. You might say something like, "I'm ready and eager to reengage with work and would love to share with you some examples from my prior job that I think will help me to be successful in this role. For example . . ."

Check for a values match

In the end, a company that is not understanding of your taking time out of the workforce for caregiving responsibilities is probably not a place where you'd want to work. Any job interview is a two-way meeting. Have ready some questions that will help you assess if the values of the organization are a fit for you. Thornton has noticed that candidates are now making more values-based decisions. "The candidates are testing executives more than executives are testing candidates," she said. "And candidates are testing for 'How are you going to handle this when I throw you this curveball? What did you do in Black Lives Matter, and does that align with me?' They're looking much more holistically at 'What team am I joining?' than they were before."

Looking for companies that have return-to-work programs is also a good screening mechanism and a potentially good way to rejoin the workforce. CommonSpirit Health has launched a Boomerang campaign targeted at people who have left the workforce during the pandemic. The aim is to get them back into the workforce, whether the work is full-time, part-time, or some other flexible arrangement. Likewise, in 2008, Goldman Sachs developed a traditional return-to-work program for people who have been out of the paid workforce for two or more years. The company has more recently launched a separate Covid-19 Career Relaunch Initiative for people who left the workforce after March 2020 because of the pandemic.

Get support

Conducting a job search is invariably full of challenges, which can feel even bigger after you take an extended leave. A coach, a therapist, a job-search work group, or all of these can be good sources of support beyond family and friends and can help you deal with the challenges you're likely to face along the way. These may range from addressing questions of identity that may arise, managing frustration and gaining momentum when you feel stuck, or handling more tactical job-search questions. Cole-Frieman said, "I encourage people to have that group of people you can go to when you get to that point where you say, 'Oh, this isn't working,' so you can get that pep talk to get back in the ring and try again, because it can be hard." Section 3 offers practical ways to assemble a team of advocates, including mentors, partners, in-house peers, and outside colleagues and friends.

. . .

Returning to the workforce after taking time out for caregiving doesn't have to be as daunting as it might otherwise be. Using the six preceding strategies can help you merge back on the career highway more smoothly and get the results you're looking for.

Adapted from content posted on hbr.org, December 3, 2021 (product #H06PZH).

18

A Detour Doesn't Have to Compromise Your Goals

by Dorie Clark

For almost every professional, there are times when your career path deviates from what you might have hoped. For instance, you might face a layoff, a reassignment, a relocation, or the need to take time off for health issues or caregiving.

In the short term, the situation is clear: If you or another member of your household has lost a job, someone needs to make up for the lost income. If your kids cannot attend school in person, then someone has to stay home with them and supervise their virtual learning. And if you're the primary caregiver to children or other family members, you need to ensure you have the flexibility at work to handle any situation that comes your way at home.

Unfortunately, meeting those urgent needs sometimes means that longer-range goals get set aside. Many people find themselves turning down coveted promotions to maintain flexible hours. Or they accept positions in fields they actually want to leave or say yes to jobs they're overqualified for or unexcited about, because they simply need the money.

Those decisions—while painful—may be necessary in the short term. But a temporary departure from your professional goals doesn't mean that all is lost. It's essential—and possible, even with a busy day job—to stay focused on your long-term career trajectory so that you can rebound quickly and get back on a path that feels right for you.

In conducting research for my book *The Long Game: How to Be a Long-Term Thinker in a Short-Term World*, I discovered a variety of ways that professionals faced with these trade-offs can begin to take back control over their career arc. Here are four strategies you can employ.

Reframe the situation

No one enjoys feeling as if they're stalled or moving backward professionally. Indeed, research by Harvard Business School professor Teresa Amabile shows that one of the most powerful indicators of employees' mood and satisfaction is the feeling that they're making progress toward a meaningful goal. If you view your career decisions as part of a regression, you're almost certainly going to feel frustrated, angry, or ashamed. Instead, broaden your view: Your job isn't the only element of your life, and even if you're temporarily making less progress on the career front, you're advancing other goals that you've previously identified as equally or even more important. For example, you are providing for your family economically or spending more time with them.

Dig to identify learning opportunities

If your current job isn't exactly what you're looking for, it's easy to write it off as something you're doing just for the money. But even suboptimal situations can become powerful opportunities to develop your skills if you recognize them and leverage them as a chance to learn. For instance, one leader I know is hesitant to leave her job amid economic uncertainty. She is leaning into her strained relationship with a querulous colleague and consciously attempting to get better at dealing with difficult people. Similarly, you might uncover hidden opportunities to develop new aspects of the job that align better with your interests (for instance, research into new technology) or that enable you to build your network.

Push back against standard options

The choice may seem stark: Pursue your dreams, or succumb to necessity. But if we get creative, we often see many more possibilities than we might have imagined (and certainly more than we're initially presented with). For instance, one client I work with is a nascent entrepreneur whose new business was hit hard by the pandemic. Faced with pressing financial needs—and a friend who wanted to hire him—he debated giving up his business and accepting a corporate job similar to the one he'd left a year earlier. After our discussion, he realized that those weren't the only two options. He's now in talks with his friend about the possibility of converting the job offer into a consulting contract, which would give him the security he needs while building his new business, thereby allowing him to pursue his entrepreneurial vision. Remember, there are almost always more than two choices, and most offers can be negotiated.

Finally, harness small amounts of time toward your goals

As you make your way through life and your career, it's likely you'll go through a period where you're feeling burned out and overextended. Under those circumstances, it may feel like a pipe dream to carve out time for long-term professional development. But even small increments of time can be valuable if we harness them properly.

For instance, if you listen to a professional development podcast or an audiobook instead of music while you're exercising or running errands, you will have "read" dozens more books over a year. And one technique that notoriously productive Wharton professor Adam Grant employs is to use the handful of minutes between meetings—which often get lost to chitchat or social media—to make progress on microgoals he's working on. Your leveraging a spare three minutes to send a networking email or to download a few articles on a topic you're researching may seem insignificant, but as Amabile's aforementioned research on progress and employee satisfaction shows, even these tiny steps forward can create a feeling of momentum—which is essential to staying positive during a tour of duty in a job one doesn't love.

. . .

It's easy to become self-critical when things don't go according to plan. But by following these four strategies—and coupling them with a dose of grace and self-compassion—you can accomplish what needs to happen now and prepare yourself for the future you've envisioned.

Adapted from "A Career Detour Doesn't Have to Compromise Your Long-Term Goals," on hbr.org, March 29, 2021.

19

When a Major Life Change Upends Your Sense of Self

by Madeline Toubiana, Trish Ruebottom, and Luciana Turchick Hakak

Human beings have a complicated relationship with change. While it is both inevitable and essential for growth, change can also be deeply uncomfortable—especially if it feels involuntary or out of our control.

As researchers focused on social change, our group has spent the last 10 years studying how people react to drastic changes in their lives. We've conducted hundreds of interviews with people who lost a desired identity, such as former white-collar professionals forced to move into lower-status careers, and people trying to shed an undesirable or stigmatized identity, such as former prisoners working to reintegrate themselves in their communities.[1] Interestingly, regardless of whether the changes were ostensibly positive or negative, many of the people we talked to struggled to move on from their past identities and embrace their new selves. This sense of being stuck—a phenomenon we call *identity paralysis*—often left people feeling angry, frustrated, and hopeless about their current situations.

However, we also found that some people avoided identity paralysis by taking these major life changes in stride and embracing their new roles with positivity. Through our interviews, we identified five strategies that can help anyone come to terms with a new identity (whether you're happy about the change or not) and move forward on a path of identity growth rather than identity paralysis:

Mark a distinct break with the past

Even if we logically know that our situation has changed, it can be difficult to get that change to really sink in. Many of our interviewees described a key event that "flipped a switch" for them: a tipping point that empowered them to make (and truly accept) a change. For example, some participants who were trying to leave behind stigmatized pasts spoke about the significance of a specific milestone, such as a birthday or the birth of a child, in helping them embrace their new identities. One person told us how after two days in the hospital, he decided that the moment he woke up would be his rebirth, explaining that the experience marked the end of his past in a symbolically meaningful way.

To be clear, the actual event that marks the break is not what is important. Rather, the people we interviewed expressed a strong need for something that symbolically represented the end of a chapter in their life. Our finding is consistent with prior work on the power of symbolic shifts: For example, in her influential books *Out of the Cloister* and *Becoming an Ex*, Catholic nun-turned-sociologist Helen Ebaugh explains that even after making the decision to leave the convent, it was the moment of physically taking off the habit and donning laywomen's clothes that marked the transition for many former nuns and allowed them to leave their old identities behind.

So, if you're struggling to disentangle your past and present selves, see if you can define a moment that can be imbued with significance, and articulate that to yourself and those around you. Simply recognizing a specific moment as a divider between the past and the present can help you extricate yourself from an identity that is no longer relevant to your life.

Craft a story to tie the past and present together

Of course, marking a distinct break with the past doesn't make the past disappear—nor should it. Your past is a part of you, and a new identity can only take hold if it's connected to your prior identities. Consequently, it is important to link your present with your past by creating a narrative that's compelling, believable, and easy to share with others.

For example, we spoke with an immigrant who was forced to give up his career as a civil engineer and become a taxi driver. When he told the story to himself and to others, he framed it around a narrative of parental sacrifice, explaining that he took on the new role for his children. He described how happy he was for his kids, explaining that setting up their lives at the expense of his own was a trade he was more than willing to make. A former banker took a similar approach to framing his story, expressing confidence that immigrating was "a very good decision, believe me. Not for myself, [but for] my family, my sons and daughter. They're very happy. Everybody is married. They have a happy life. Everybody has their children. They are going to school. They're happy."

Conversely, many of the interviewees we spoke with who came from troubled or stigmatized pasts embraced the narrative of the prodigal son or a fallen angel. In different ways, they explained how darkness led them to light, how their new and promising paths forward would have been impossible without starting from their prior identities. We found that those who could tell their own stories in a way that aligned with a widely recognizable narrative were better able to make peace with their transitions and leave behind their old identities, expressing more positive sentiment about their current situations than did those who did not develop such stories.

Acknowledge and work through challenging emotions

Part of what makes identity paralysis so difficult to overcome is that it isn't just your idea of who you are that gets stuck in the past. It can also cause you to get stuck in the emotions associated with that past. Whether you're ashamed of a prior role or decision, angry about the circumstances that led to your current situation, or feeling hopeless, scared, or any other challenging negative emotion, getting stuck in these feelings can block your transition (even if you are ready for it cognitively).

To be sure, working on how you think about yourself is certainly an important component of making an identity transition. But this emphasis on the cognitive aspect can often leave the emotional side undervalued. Even if you have decided rationally that you want to move on, emotions can linger—and getting stuck in powerful negative emotions such as shame or anger can be paralyzing. Our identities are shaped by how we feel about them, so to make a successful transition, we have to acknowledge and actively work on our emotions. As one interviewee explained, "No one is going to break the cycle until they accept who they are, and what they are, and what they've done, and they forgive themselves. You can't move forward unless you forgive yourself. A lot of people don't know that. So they live in guilt and shame for so long."

Across our interviews, we found that the people who were best able to embrace their new identities were those who recognized the emotions holding them back and proactively worked through those feelings. Many strategies can help you transform negative emotions, but we found that one of the most effective strategies is to intentionally activate an opposing, positive emotion. For example, one worker who was forced to change careers because of an injury described how she moved past her shame by focusing on her pride in how she had established and was running her own business. Importantly, it's not about pushing negative emotions away—rather, moving forward necessitates truly acknowledging these difficult feelings and then refocusing on more-helpful ones.

Focus on meaningful non-work-related identities

It's easy to feel as though your job is your whole identity—especially when you just lost a great job or when it feels as if the only thing anyone sees when they look at you is your job. But research has shown that it's very possible to have multiple, coexisting identities at the same time.[2] For this reason, if you're uncomfortable with your current identity at work, focusing on other aspects of your identity can be an effective strategy to help you get through a difficult transition.

For example, a woman who had left sex work explained that it was important to her that she was "able to be a mum now and spend time with my kids." Some of the immigrant professionals we interviewed who were struggling with downward occupational transitions also described how they felt better after leaning into their parental roles. Instead of focusing on their discontentment with their current jobs or on their resentment at having to give up their past careers, they found meaning in defining themselves by their roles as providers.

Similarly, a former prisoner described how the simple act being a good uncle by playing soccer with his nephew helped him move past his negative self-image and envision a better version of himself. Others focused more on their roles in their communities, on volunteer positions, or on activism. Reminding yourself of your full range of identities can help you focus on the positive, realize that you're more than what you do (or used to do), and keep moving forward.

Don't be afraid to fantasize

While focusing on the concrete positives in your life can be helpful, our research also revealed that there is great power in the imaginary. This finding is consistent with prior research on the concept of *postalgia*, which refers to a yearning not for an idealized version of the past but for a similarly utopic future.[3] In our interviews, we found that some of the people who were most comfortable in their new identities imagined that their current circumstances were only a stepping-stone on the path to their ultimate (if objectively unrealistic) future.

Surprisingly, this strategy still seemed to work even if the world they imagined was truly a fantasy: an abstract future they could daydream about, often with little basis in reality. Rather than detailing specific plans or tactics to realize these dreams, the participants who took this approach fantasized about an alternative future as if it would definitely happen, despite seeming to have no intention of actually pursuing it.

For example, one interviewee who was forced to shift from his job as a network engineer to become a taxi driver explained why he felt good about his situation: "In the future, I have plans to get a computer job. Not now, maybe after 10 years, 20 years, then I'll definitely go for my own business." He was in his third year of driving a taxi and had no tangible plans to move into tech—and yet the vague possibility of a brighter future made the present more palatable. Similarly, many people enjoy window-shopping or browsing vacation spots online, wistfully imagining an experience that they're unlikely to ever have. It may seem counterintuitive, but our research suggests that in moderation, this kind of daydreaming can be an effective means of coping with a challenging situation and getting mentally unstuck.

Of course, these findings should not be misconstrued as an argument against working to improve a bad situation. But the practical work of planning and implementing positive change can be draining, time-consuming, and, if overdone, paralyzing. Balancing the difficult tasks of accepting and improving reality with a healthy dose of fantasy can be critical in ensuring that you stay motivated.

. . .

Whether you're taking on a new role, shifting careers, or going through a major life change like those experienced by the people in our interviews, it's never easy to let go of a past identity. But left unchecked, identity paralysis can threaten both your career prospects and your mental health. To avoid getting stuck and to truly move forward in your life, you'll want to acknowledge and embrace your current identity, your past self, and everything in between.

Adapted from content posted on hbr.org, January 28, 2022 (product #H06U7Z).

20

Learn to Get Better at Transitions

by Avivah Wittenberg-Cox

There is a small, disheveled baby robin taking its very first steps in my garden today. It looks a bit dazed and exhausted, its lovely yellow down all awry. I know exactly what it feels like. The young bird looks like a lot of people I know right now. At almost every age, everyone seems to be on the cusp of a similar transition: taking their first steps into an uncertain and illegible new world. As I write this, World War II planes fly overhead to celebrate Queen Elizabeth's official birthday. Like my own mother, who shares her birthday, she is turning 93. They are both remarkably well and not finished with transitions.

At just shy of 57, I feel poised between these two ends of the spectrum: the baby bird and the great-grandmother.

From this middle spot, I can observe my entire family hanging, in a seemingly collective cliff ritual, on the edge of change. We are all making the transition—quasi-simultaneously and quite unexpectedly—into our next chapters. My daughter is graduating from college. My son is starting his first company. My husband is adapting to something he resists calling retirement. My mother has just been fitted with her first hearing aids and is suddenly complaining about the noise of the sirens in the city. Not to mention my trio of good friends, one who lost a job, one who moved countries, and one who split from her partner.

Every one of this cross-generational crew is struggling to let go of *what was* (identity, community, colleagues, and competencies) to embrace *what's next* (as-yet unknown, undefined, and ambiguous). There is a mixture of fear ("Who am I?") and excitement ("I am *so* ready for a change"), confusion ("What do I want?") and certainty ("Time to move on").

Because more of us are living longer, healthier lives, we'll face more of these moments of liminality. And so I'm sitting in the garden, watching Robin Jr. test its fledgling wings, researching how to prepare for the several decades still ahead. No matter where we are in our own journeys, we could all get better at the skill of transitioning. To do this, we should focus on four component skills.

Pacing and Planning

Longevity means that, more than ever, we need to plan for change. Using the gift of decades requires acknowledging their existence and deciding what you want to do with them. People say you can't have it all, but the gift of time gives us new options to have a lot more than we ever thought possible.

- Measure out your life to date in major chapters. Developmental psychologist Erik Erikson mapped out adulthood in seven-year periods. What were the highlights, accomplishments, and lessons of each of your past seven-year periods?
- How many seven-year periods do you have before you hit 100?
- Draw a timeline from zero to 100, and place yourself on it. This gives you an idea of the possible length of the road ahead.

Leaving Gracefully

There comes a time in jobs, life phases, or relationships where you know an arc has reached its end. Knowing when it is time to end—and ending well—will become an increasingly valuable skill as lives lengthen and as transitions multiply across both personal and professional lives. Endings can come from within, the result of burnout, boredom, depression, or exhaustion. Or they can come from without, the land of restructurings, layoffs, divorce, or other major life shifts. These endings are the prequel to re-creation. An ending is not always an easy time—for anyone involved, at work or at home. We can spend quite a lot of it loitering unproductively, wondering whether we should stay or go. But good endings are the best building blocks to good beginnings.

- Choosing to choose gives you agency. The choice itself, sometimes made years before you actually move, is the first and often the biggest step.

- Ask yourself if you are staying where you are out of love or out of fear. Do you love where you are, or do you fear leaving it for a murky unknown? Murkiness is a lousy state to live in, but many of us stay stuck here. "Who would I be without this title, this salary, or this position?" we ask ourselves. It can be an exciting question, not a scary one.

- Embrace confusion, ambiguity, and questions. There redefinition lies. And remember, you don't have to face the uncertainty alone.

Letting the Inside Out

Self-knowledge is one of the hard-won rewards of aging. For many of us, our inner selves remain unexplored territory until the second half of adulthood. My friend Mary had yearned for creative outlets much of her life but had never considered herself artistic until she took up writing and painting in her sixties. At 80, she is a successful artist and a published poet. What part of yourself might be waiting, hidden in the wings? A few questions to set you on your way:

- What have you most enjoyed in your career to date?
- What kind of people energize you, and what kind of environments shut you down?
- Do you want to transfer skills or start from scratch and reinvent? Build on accomplishments or never hear of them again?
- What kind of balance will you prioritize for this phase? Focus on one thing or cumulate a series of side hustles into a portfolio life?
- Do you want to anchor security or toss it to the winds?

In this journey, which can take a few years, you'll want to pack a comforting "travel bag": an advisory board of trusted supporters, a realistic timeline, a financial plan, and clearly negotiated support from your partner if you have one. Rome wasn't built in a day, and preparing for the next quarter of your life requires more than updating your LinkedIn profile. Invest in the next phase as you would in any seven-year project. Seriously.

Letting the Outside In

Any transition plan will benefit from feedback from the outside world. Essentially, you are market-testing your new plan and figuring out where you are most needed and appreciated. Clare and Mark thought that when they reached their early sixties, they'd retire and leave their U.K. base to live in a new country. So, in their fifties, they took a sabbatical from work and lived in four countries for three months each to find the perfect place. In the end, this experience helped them decide to enter a new profession instead of a new country. They decided to move to a new home just an hour from where they'd been living and start an eco-friendly farm, fulfilling a long-held passion for sustainability and food.

This gathering of outside feedback is what London Business School professor Herminia Ibarra calls "outsight"—physically visiting these metaphorical new lands to discover not only what you love but also where you are loved. Her point is that insight alone may not be enough.

- What do others most appreciate about you?
- Which of your accomplishments or activities elicit the best response or the most appreciation or follow-up?
- Which of your experiments have attracted the kind of questions, people, or projects that excite you?
- When, where, and with whom did you feel most alive?

Leaping

People who have successfully made the transition to a new phase and invested in something they deeply care about, sometimes for the first time in their lives, are an inspiring sight. Some people only find, or allow themselves to find, their calling after they've fulfilled all their duties—to their own earlier expectations, to parents, to family. The freedom that comes from finally aligning with yourself is profound. Neither fame nor fortune can feed the unsatisfied soul. As Erich Fromm wrote half a century ago, "The whole life of the individual is nothing but the process of giving birth to himself; indeed, we should be fully born when we die—although it is the tragic fate of most individuals to die before they are born."[1]

Now that we have a few extra decades to test our wings, the real challenge may be remembering that it's never too late to fly.

Adapted from content posted on hbr.org, July 5, 2018 (product #H04FD4).

NOTES

Chapter 8

1. Cynthia Hess, Tanima Ahmed, and Jeff Hayes, "Providing Unpaid Household and Care Work in the United States: Uncovering Inequality," briefing paper C487, Institute for Women's Policy Research, January 2020, https://iwpr.org/wp-content/uploads/2020/01/IWPR-Providing-Unpaid-Household-and-Care-Work-in-the-United-States-Uncovering-Inequality.pdf.

2. Kathryn Heath, "3 Simple Ways for Women to Rethink Office Politics and Wield More Influence at Work," hbr.org, December 18, 2017, https://hbr.org/2017/12/3-simple-ways-for-women-to-rethink-office-politics-and-wield-more-influence-at-work.

3. Shawn Achor, "Do Women's Networking Events Move the Needle on Equality?," hbr.org, February 13, 2018, https://hbr.org/2018/02/do-womens-networking-events-move-the-needle-on-equality?

4. Alex M. Wood, Alex P. Linley, John Maltby, Michael Baliousis, and Stephen Joseph, "The Authentic Personality: A Theoretical and Empirical Conceptualization and the Development of the Authenticity Scale," *Journal of Counseling Psychology* 55, no. 3 (2008): 385–399, https://psycnet.apa.org/record/2008-09087-008.

5. Jessica Nordell, "This Is How Everyday Sexism Could Stop You from Getting That Promotion," *New York Times*, October 14, 2021, https://www.nytimes.com/interactive/2021/10/14/opinion/gender-bias.html.

6. Gregory M. Walton and Geoffrey L. Cohn, "A Question of Belonging: Race, Social Fit, and Achievement," *Journal of Personality and Social Psychology* 92, no. 1 (2007): 82–96, https://psycnet.apa.org/record/2006-23056-007.

Chapter 9

1. Linda Babcock, Maria P. Recalde, Lise Vesterlund, and Laurie Weingart, "Gender Differences in Accepting and Receiving Requests for Tasks with Low Promotability," *American Economic Review* 107, no. 3 (2017): 714–747, https://pubs.aeaweb.org/doi/pdfplus/10.1257/aer.20141734.

Chapter 11

1. Carla Harris, "How to Find the Person Who Can Help You Get Ahead at Work," filmed November 30, 2018 at TEDWomen 2018, Palm Springs, CA, video, https://www.ted.com/talks/carla_harris_how_to_find_the_person_who_can_help_you_get_ahead_at_work.
2. Sylvia Ann Hewlett and Kennedy Ihezie, "Sponsoring a Protégé Remotely," July 2, 2020, hbr.org, https://hbr.org/2020/07/sponsoring-a-protege-remotely.

Chapter 17

1. M. E. Heilman and T. G. Okimoto, "Motherhood: A Potential Source of Bias in Employment Decisions," *Journal of Applied Psychology* 93, no. 1 (2008): 189–198, https://psycnet.apa.org/doiLanding?doi=10.1037%2F0021-9010.93.1.189.

Chapter 19

1. Madeline Toubiana, "Once in Orange Always in Orange? Identity Paralysis and the Enduring Influence of Institutional Logics on Identity," *Academy of Management Journal* 63, no. 6 (December 9, 2020), https://doi.org/10.5465/amj.2017.0826.

2. Glen E. Kreiner, Elaine C. Hollensbe, and Mathew L. Sheep, "On the Edge of Identity: Boundary Dynamics at the Interface of Individual and Organizational Identities," *Human Relations* 59, no. 10 (October 1, 2006): 1315–1341, https://journals.sagepub.com/doi/10.1177/0018726706071525.

3. Sierk Ybema, "Talk of Change; Temporal Contrasts and Collective Identities," *Organization Studies* 31, no. 4 (June 2, 2010): 481–503, https://doi.org/10.1177/0170840610372205.

Chapter 20

1. Erich Fromm, *The Sane Society* (New York: Holt, Rinehart and Winston, 1955), 16.

INDEX

Aboubaker, Mimi, 27–38
Abrams, Stacey, 39–46
accomplishments
  celebrating, in burnout prevention, 8
  talking with your boss about your team's work and, 51–52
  validating yourself for, 53
adrenaline trap, 11
Amabile, Teresa, 166, 169
ambition
  changing mindsets about women showing, 83–85
  moving up in organizations and, 63, 64
ambition trap, 10
Amico, Laura, 5–9
Angelou, Maya, 104
appreciation
  not feeling valued at work, 49–50
  raising your profile for, 54–55
  recognizing others' contributions and, 52–53, 55
  talking with your boss about not getting, 51
assertiveness
  balancing with persuasion, 58–62
  office politics and, 76
authenticity
  office politics and lack of, 75
  requirements for, 80
authenticity trap, 21–22
avoiders, in job searches, 27

Babcock, Linda, 87–94
Bakare, Lola, 98, 99
being indispensable, 95–100
  being less available to avoid, 96–97
  example of, 95–96
  helping to find your successor and, 99–100
  moving to another role and, 98–99
  ways of saying no to, 97–98
  ways to avoid, 96–100
Bernstein, Amy, xi–xv, 39, 40, 42, 57–64, 149–156

Bezos, Jeff, 109
bonding capital, in networks, 132
bosses
  asking for help from, in job searches, 22
  looking for possibilities to expand your work role and, 18
  negotiating about job titles with, 69–70
  talking with about not feeling valued at work, 51
  talking with about your team's achievements, 51–52
  See also managers
bridging capital, in networks, 132
Brockway, Anna, 54–55
burnout, 5–9
business needs, and taking time off between jobs, 141–142
business ownership
  confronting self-doubt and fears in, 43–44
  strengths and weaknesses of being a woman and, 44–46
busyness trap, 10

Cable, Dan, 66, 67, 69–70
career
  advice for early period of, 57–64
  asking for help in, 22
  asking for a job title in, 65–72
  building meaningful connections in, 103–112
  career guide for building, 3–18
  impact of being indispensable on, 95–100
  playing office politics during, 73–86
  preventing burnout in, 5–9
  questions for navigating the second half of, 19–25
  staying too long in a role and, 96
  taking on too many non-promotable tasks and impact on, 87–94
  taking ownership of your learning in, 16–17
  talking about with your mentor, 116–117
career and personal manifesto, 28–38
  engage step in, 30–35
  evaluate step in, 28–30
  execute step in, 35–38
  three steps in creating, 28
career champions, in the second half of your career, 23
career detours, 165–169
  carving out professional development time in, 168–169
  finding creative options in, 167–168
  identifying learning opportunities in, 167
  making progress toward goals during, 166–167, 168–169

reframing the situation in, 166–167
career exploration, taking time off between jobs for, 139–140
career guide, 3–18
defining your purpose in, 11–13
documenting skills and creating a selling statement in, 13–15
four steps in creating, 4
goal of, 4
seizing opportunities to expand yourself and, 15–18
writing down your career traps in, 4–11
career traps, 4–11
caregiving breaks
asking about company policies on, 162
being transparent about, 159
getting support for job searches after, 163
not dwelling on the time gap in, 161
sharing about what you learned during, 160–161
showing yourself some compassion during, 158–159
strategies for reentering the workforce after, 157–163
Caulfield, Emily, 39, 40, 42–43, 44, 149, 151–152, 155
champions, in the second half of your career, 23
change
reactions to and moving on from, 171–172
See also life changes; transitions
Charles, Ray, 104
chemistry with mentors, 116, 123–130
description of, 123–124
knowing when the chemistry exactly there, 127–128
questions to help identify, 125–127
reasons for needing for full potential, 124–125
ways of finding, 128–129
chronic illnesses, time off for, 149–156
fear and anxiety about sharing about, 150–151, 155
managers and, 152–154
planning for and communicating about time, 156
timing of disclosing information about, 151–152
Clark, Dorie, 131–135, 165–169
coaching, and navigating the second half of your career, 19–25
Cohen, Paige, 57–64
Cole-Frieman, Wanda, 158–159, 160–161, 163
comfort, with mentors, 125

compensation
evaluating in job searches, 29
job titles and, 66, 67
taking time off between jobs and, 143–144
competition, and women and office politics, 75
competitors, 109–110
confidence
being assertive and, 59
impact of staying too long in a role, 96
receiving feedback and, 62
connection, with mentors, 126
connections
competitors, 109–110
mentees, 110–111
mentors, 104–106
partners, 108–109
sponsors, 106–108
connectors, in the second half of your career, 23
Coqual, 106
Covey, Stephen, 110
Covid pandemic, 6, 145, 162
C-suite, setting yourself up for, 62–64
curiosity for learning, as entrepreneurship quality, 39–40

decompression time, between jobs, 145–146
DeSantis, Christy, 97
development, investing in your own, 16–17
Diamond, Julie, 73–86
Dillon, Karen, 50, 51–52, 53
diversity, in network membership, 131–135
diversity of thought, in partnerships, 42

Edwards, Laurie, 149–156
Ellis, Sarah, 16–17
emotional support system, in the second half of your career, 23
engage step, in creating a career and personal manifesto, 30–35
entrepreneurship, personal qualities brought to, 39–40
environment, evaluating in job searches, 28
evaluate step, in creating a career and personal manifesto, 28–30
execute step, in creating a career and personal manifesto, 35–38
expectations
about being available, 96–97
about taking on non-promotable tasks, 91–92
about women running businesses, 45
expectation trap, 10

family
caregiving breaks for, 157–163
cross-generational changes in, 181–182 (*see also* transitions)
taking time off between jobs for, 144–145
fears, confronting in business, 43–44
feedback
being assertive in reaction to, 60–62
lack of, and not feeling valued at work, 50
from mentors, 127–128
sources of, in the second half of your career, 23
Fernandez, Jenny, xiv, 103–112
finances, and burnout, 5–6
financial considerations, in taking time off between jobs, 143–144
Fromm, Erich, 187–188

Gallo, Amy, 63
Gates, Bill, 109
gatherers, in job searches, 27
gender
assertiveness and, 58–59
caregiving breaks and, 157
political skills and, 75
problem-solving perspectives and, 45
starting businesses and, 44–45
gender gap, in leadership, 73
Gibbings, Michelle, 3–18
glass ceilings, 42
Glassdoor, 67
goals
career detours and, 166–167, 168–169
job satisfaction and progress toward, 166, 169
Goldman Sachs, 162
Grant, Adam, 169
group mentoring, 130
growth mindset, 84–85

Hakak, Luciana Turchick, 171–179
Harris, Carla, 106
health care coverage, and taking time off between jobs, 143, 144
health reasons, time off for, 149–156
fear and anxiety about sharing about, 150–151, 155
managers and, 152–154
planning for and communicating about, 156
timing of disclosing information about, 151–152
help, asking for, in your job search, 22
Hodgson, Lara, 39–46
honesty, in partnerships, 41
Horoszowski, Mark, 119
"How Woman Manage the Gendered Norms of Leadership" (Zheng, Kark, and Meister), 58

Ibarra, Herminia, 186
identity paralysis, 172
acknowledging and working through emotions from, 175–176
activating positive emotions to transform negative emotions in, 176
focusing on non-work-related identities in, 176–177
imagining a new future identity in, 177–179
strategies for moving forward from, 172–179

jobs
setting yourself up for the C-suite, 62–64
taking time off between, 139–147
Jobs, Steve, 109
job satisfaction, and progress toward goals, 166, 169
job searches
approaches when you don't know what you want to do next, 27–38
avoiding advice of convenience in, 31
asking for help in, 22
categories job seekers in, 27
job search prioritization matrix used in, 29–33
opportunities prioritization matrix used in, 35–37
people to reach out to for advice in, 31–35
questions for navigating the second half of your career and, 19–25
reentering the workforce after a caregiving break and, 157–163
writing a career and personal manifesto in, 28–38
job search prioritization matrix, 29–33
evaluation categories in, 29–30
example of, 32–33
opportunities prioritization matrix using results from, 36
questions to help in filling out, 28–29
job titles, 65–72
being appreciative in ongoing discussions about, 70–71
case study of, 71–72
compensation and, 66, 67
organizational hierarchy related to, 67–68
impact of, 66
listening to others' perspectives on, 68–69
as part of multi-issue discussions, 68
reflecting on your reasons behind wanting a new title, 66–67
strategizing before meeting about, 69

ways of approaching the conversation with your boss about, 69–70
Joffe, Rosalind, 151
Jones, Quincy, 104
Journal of Happiness Studies, 145

Kark, Ronit, 58
Knight, Rebecca, 49–55, 65–72

leadership development programs, 79–80
leadership role
gender gap in, 73
setting yourself up for, 62–64
learning
during career detours, 167
during caregiving breaks, 160–161
creating a collective curriculum for, 17
curiosity and zest for, in entrepreneurship, 39–40
experimenting as part of, 17
learning from others as part of, 16
preparing for the second half of your career using, 24–25
taking ownership of, 16–17
learning communities, creating, 16
Level Up (Abrams and Hodgson), 42–43
life changes, 171–179
acknowledging and working through emotions from, 175–176
activating positive emotions to transform negative emotions in, 176
crafting a story to tie past and present together in, 173–174
examples of events precipitating, 171
focusing on non-work-related identities in, 176–177
imagining a new future identity in, 177–179
making a distinct break with the past in, 172–173
reactions to and moving on from, 171–172
strategies for moving forward from, 172–179
See also transitions
LinkedIn, 34, 67, 105, 159, 186
adding your selling statement to, 15

Mallick, Mita, 95–100
managers
needing time off for health reasons and, 152–154
See also bosses
Markman, Art, 5–9
McKee, Annie, 49, 50, 51–52, 53–54
meetings
first, with your mentor, 114–116
practicing what you want to say before, 59

Meister, Alyson, 58
mentees, 110–111
mentoring
  alternative approaches to, 129
  companies' traditional approach of pairing people in, 128
  group, 130
  peer-to-peer, 129
mentors, 104–106
  asking for a first meeting with, 114–116
  benefits of, 114
  building chemistry with, 116, 123–130
  building strong bonds with, 105–106
  clicking or clashing issues in, 126–127
  example email for contacting, 115
  expressing gratitude to, 121–122
  feeling comfortable with, 125
  feeling connection with, 126
  finding, 113–122
  following up and scheduling more meetings with, 118–120
  keeping updated on your activities, 120–21
  maintaining your relationship with, 120–122
  making a clear request for a regular relationship with, 119
  nurturing your relationship with, 116–120
  offering to help your mentor, 121
  people who are different from yourself as, 129
  in the second half of your career, 23
  sending a thank-you note after the initial meeting, 117
  taking the time for getting to know, 116–117
  transparency about your intentions with, 127
Mones, Lesli, 73–86
Musk, Elon, 109

narratives, to tie past and present together during life changes, 173–174
Neale, Margaret, 65–66, 66–67, 67–68, 69, 70–71
Neale, Palena, xiii, 19–25
Neff, Kristin, 158
negotiations
  about job titles, 65–72
  for time off between jobs, 140–141
networking, as a shared, reciprocal activity, 24
networks
  adding people outside your industry to, 131–135
  asking for recommendations for additions to, 134
  balance of bonding and bridging capital on, 132

best reason for building diversity in, 135
not looking for immediate returns on, 134–135
risk of being too narrow with members of, 131–132
scheduling time for, 133–134
strategies for diversifying, 132–135
taking an inventory of existing connections in, 133
See also support teams
No Club, The (Babcock, Peyser, Vesterlund, and Weingart), 88
non-promotable tasks (NPTs), 87–94
characteristics of, 89–90
evaluating consequences of taking on, 92–94
examples of, 87, 88
gender differences in expectations about handling, 88–89
reasons people feel pressured to take on, 90–92
Nooyi, Indra, 109

office politics, 73–86
definition of, 73
five reasons why women dislike, 74–76
five ways to shift your mindset about, 76–86
penalties for women showing skills in, 76, 83
stress from engaging in, 74
women's aversion to, 73–74
Olvera-Marshall, Lourdes, 142, 144
Omadeke, Janice, 123–130
opportunities, evaluating in job searches, 29
opportunities prioritization matrix, 35–37
example of, 36–37
how to use, 35–36
priority quadrants in, 36
outsights, in transitions, 186–187

partners, 108–109
partnerships
confronting self-doubt and fears in, 43–44
qualities needed in, 40–42
strengths and weaknesses of being a woman in, 44–46
transparency in, 41
peer-to-peer mentoring, 129
personal needs, and taking time off between jobs, 144–145
persuasion, balancing with assertiveness, 58–62
Peyser, Brenda, 87–94
Phan, Janet T., 113–122
planning
longevity and transitions and, 183
for time off for health reasons, 156

podcasts, for professional development, 168–169
political skills
organizational life and, 74
penalties for women having, 76, 83
See also office politics
postalgia, 177–178
power tactics, changing mindsets about, 81–83
problem-solving, and gender, 45
professional development, and career detours, 168–169
purpose, defining, for your career guide, 11–13
Putnam, Robert, 132

race
political skills and, 75
women starting businesses and, 44–45
Ranieri, Anna, 64
Rees, Rhonda, 71–72
relationship audit, in the second half of your career, 23
relationships
competitors, 109–110
mentees, 110–111
mentors, 104–106
partners, 108–109
sponsors, 106–108
resilience
burnout prevention and, 7–8
as entrepreneurship quality, 40
résumé
detailing caregiving breaks on, 159
evaluating in job searches, 29
retirement benefits, and taking time off between jobs, 143, 144
retirement goals, and burnout, 5–6
Rosenfeld, Irene, 109
Ruebottom, Trish, 171–179

Sandberg, Sheryl, 104
savings, and burnout, 5–6
schedules
carving out professional development time on, 168–169
needing time off for health reasons and, 153
putting networking time on, 133–134
taking on non-promotable tasks and, 93–94
Self-Compassion (Neff), 158
self-doubt
not feeling valued at work and, 50
women in business and, 43
selling statement
creating, 14–15
uses for, 15
7 Habits of Highly Effective People, The (Covey), 110
skills
developing during career detours, 167
documenting for your career guide, 13–14

evaluating in job searches, 29
moving to the next step and, 64
non-promotable tasks and, 90
updating, for the second half of your career, 24–25
social change, reactions to, 171
sponsor effect, 106–107
sponsors, 106–108
Stokes, Caroline, 145
stories, to tie past and present together during life changes, 173–174
Summers, Larry, 104
support teams
adding people outside your industry to, 131–135
building and accessing, in the second half of your career, 23–24
building meaningful connections as part of, 103–112
job searches after caregiving breaks and, 163
mentors on (*see* mentors)
transitions and, 185–186

teams, increasing visibility of, 51–52
Thornton, Sally, 141, 142, 146–147, 158, 162
thought partners, in job searches, 30
time off between jobs, 139–147
benefit of, 139
budgeting time for ramping up at the end of, 146–147
business needs and, 141–142
factors to consider with, 141–147
financial considerations in, 143–144
giving appropriate notice with, 142–143
negotiating, 140–141
personal needs and, 144–145
taking time to decompress during, 145–146
time off for caregiving breaks
asking about company policies on, 162
being transparent about, 159
getting support for job searches after, 163
not dwelling on the time gap in, 161
sharing about what you learned during, 160–161
showing yourself some compassion during, 158–159
strategies for reentering the workforce after, 157–163
time off for health reasons, 149–156
fear and anxiety about sharing about, 150–151, 155
managers and, 152–154
planning for and communicating about, 156
timing of disclosing information about, 151–152
Toubiana, Madeline, 171–179

transitions, 181–188
exploring your inner selves during, 185–186
leaving gracefully in, 183–184
outsights in, 186–187
pacing and planning for, 183
See also life changes
translation trap, 10–11
transparency
with mentors about your intentions, 127
in partnerships, 41
reentering the workforce after a caregiving break and, 159
in showcasing your work, 55
trust, in partnerships, 41–42
Tupper, Helen, 16–17
Twitter, reaching out to professionals on for job search advice, 34–35

Vesterlund, Lise, xiv, 87–94, 103–112

Weingart, Laurie, 87–94
Winfrey, Oprah, 104
Wittenberg-Cox, Avivah, xv, 181–188
Women at Work podcast, 58
women of color
senior leadership and, 73
starting businesses by, 44–45
women-owned businesses
confronting self-doubt and fears in, 43–44
qualities needed in, 40–42
strengths and weaknesses of being a woman in, 44–46
work
balancing nonwork activities with, for burnout prevention, 6–7
career traps and, 4–11
combatting not feeling valued at, 49–55
delegating, during time off for health reasons, 155
finding mentorship opportunities at, 111
handling office politics at, 73–86
knowing when to move on from, 53–54
looking for possibilities to expand your role at, 18
partners at, 108–109
results of being indispensable at, 95–100
returning to, after a caregiving break, 157–163
showcasing your contributions at, 54–55
taking on too many non-promotable tasks at, 87–94
work colleagues
relationship audit of, 23
seeking support from, in the second half of your career, 24

sharing about chronic illness with, 150–151, 155
work environment, evaluating in job searches, 28
Zheng, Wei, 58
Zigarmi, Lisa, 73–86
Zucker, Rebecca, 139–147, 157–163

Discussion Guide

Since the *Women at Work* podcast first launched, we've heard from all over the world that it has inspired discussions and listening groups. We hope that this book does the same—that you'll want to share what you've learned with others. The questions in this discussion guide will help you talk about the challenges women face in the workplace and how we can work together to overcome them.

You don't need to have read the book from start to finish to participate. To get the most out of your discussion, think about the size of your group. A big group has the advantage of spreading ideas more widely—whether throughout your organization or among your friends and peers—but might lose some of the honesty and connection a small group would have. You may want to assign someone to lead the discussion to ensure that all participants are included, especially if some attendees are joining virtually. And it's a good idea to establish ground rules around privacy and confidentiality. *Women at Work* topics touch on difficult issues surrounding sexism and racism, so consider using trigger warnings.

Finally, think about what you want to accomplish in your discussion. Do you want to create a network of mutual support?

Hope to disrupt the status quo? Or are you simply looking for an empathetic ear? With your goals in mind, use the questions that follow to advance the conversation about women at work.

1. In chapter 1, Michelle Gibbings writes about the five career traps—ambition, expectation, busyness, translation, adrenaline—that can hold back your career. Can you think of a time when you experienced one of these traps? What did you to get yourself unstuck?

2. Stacey Abrams credits her successful partnership with Lara Hodgson not only to honesty but also to transparency. "Honesty is telling the truth," Abrams says. "Transparency is telling the truth before you have to." Is there space to be transparent in your workplace and with your coworkers or clients? What could you do to make your relationships more transparent? What's holding you back from making the move from honesty to transparency?

3. While being appreciated and valued for your work is a wonderful thing, you can't expect all your praise to come from external validation. In chapter 5, Rebecca Knight encourages readers to remember to regularly take the time to praise themselves. What do you do to boost your self-esteem?

4. In chapter 7, we learned the importance of a job title. As Margaret Neale says, it's not only "a signal both to the outside world and to your colleagues of what

level you are within your organization" but also an element of "your compensation package." Have you ever negotiated for a change in job title? Did the outcome positively—or negatively—affect your career? What advice would you give to others looking to negotiate their title?

5. The title of chapter 9 speaks for itself: "Are You Taking On Too Many Non-Promotable Tasks?" Do you find that women are more likely than men to take on NPTs in your organization? Are the women taking on NPTs earlier in their careers? What could you do to help change the way NPTs are distributed throughout your team or organization?

6. In chapter 11, Jenny Fernandez and Luis Velasquez say that a competitor is one of the five meaningful relationships you make in your career. The authors say that competitors can be your ally and that competition "can serve as a motivation to hone your skills and can lead to improved performance, breakthrough ideas, and a greater drive to get things done." Have you encountered a competitor during your career path? What have been the positive—or negative—outcomes of your competitive relationships?

7. In chapters 12 and 13, we learn the importance of mentorship. Have you ever had a mentor? What was it like to make your initial request? What have you done to

stay connected to your mentor and maintain a positive relationship?

8. Dorie Clark, in chapter 14, says that "it's easy to coast through life only connecting with people like ourselves. But by expending the extra effort to increase our bridging capital, we're gaining access to new insights and creating more 'career insurance' for ourselves by broadening the ranks of people who know, like, and respect our work." Have you ever networked with the intention of meeting people outside your usual groups?

9. In chapter 15, Rebecca Zucker encourages readers to take a real break before plunging into a new job so that you start off relaxed and rested. Have you ever negotiated time off before starting a new job? If so, how did you go about asking for it? What did you do with the extra time before starting your job?

10. Think back to a time when you were challenged with a career detour. How did you approach the setback? What advice would you give to a coworker or a friend who was facing a similar detour?

11. Returning to the workforce after time off can be intimidating—whether you were caregiving, recovering from an illness, or rethinking your career path. If you've returned to paid work after a break, how did others help you readjust? What can you do as a

colleague or a manager to help make someone's transition back into the workforce easier?

12. When faced with a change, we can easily slip into identity paralysis. In chapter 19, Madeline Toubiana, Trish Ruebottom, and Luciana Turchick Hakak advise, "Balancing the difficult tasks of accepting and improving reality with a healthy dose of fantasy can be critical in ensuring that you stay motivated." Take a moment to think about your wildest career fantasies. Did reflecting on your ambitions make you feel more motivated to take action and make progress on your goals?

13. There comes a time in jobs, life phases, or relationships when you know an arc has reached its end. Avivah Wittenburg-Cox, in chapter 20, argues that learning how to navigate these endings is an increasingly valuable skill. Reflect on an ending in your life. Are you proud of your response? Why or why not? What could you do next time to ensure that your ending turns into a wonderful beginning?

ABOUT THE CONTRIBUTORS

Amy Bernstein, *Women at Work* cohost, is the editor of *Harvard Business Review* and vice president and executive editorial director of Harvard Business Publishing. Follow her on Twitter @asbernstein2185.

Emily Caulfield, *Women at Work* cohost (seasons 6–7), is a freelance designer and runs a vintage clothing business, Still Cute Vintage. She was previously a senior designer at *Harvard Business Review.* Before pursuing a career in design, she held administrative roles in public education and the arts.

Mimi Aboubaker is an entrepreneur and a writer. Most recently, she founded Perfect Strangers, the largest coronavirus crisis response initiative in the United States. Prior to that, she started an edtech venture expanding access to higher education for socioeconomically disadvantaged students. For more tips on leaning in on career and life, follow her on Twitter and check out her website.

Stacey Abrams is an entrepreneur, politician, and author. She is a coauthor of *Level Up: Rise Above the Hidden Forces Holding Your Business Back* and the cofounder of Now.

Laura Amico is a senior editor at *Harvard Business Review.*

Linda Babcock is a professor of economics at Carnegie Mellon University. She is the author of *Women Don't Ask* and *Ask for It.* A behavioral economist, she is the founder and director of the Program for Research and Outreach on Gender Equity in Society, which pursues positive social change for women and girls through education, partnerships, and research.

Dorie Clark is a marketing strategist and keynote speaker who teaches at Duke University's Fuqua School of Business and has been named one of the top 50 business thinkers in the world by Thinkers50. Her latest book is *The Long Game: How to Be a Long-Term Thinker in a Short-Term World* (Harvard Business Review Press, 2021). You can receive her free Long Game strategic thinking self-assessment at dorieclark.com.

Paige Cohen (she/they) is a senior editor at Ascend.

Julie Diamond is the CEO and founder of Diamond Leadership, which provides leadership and talent development services, including coaching, consulting, assessment, and training, to its global clients. She is the author of *Power: A User's Guide.*

Laurie Edwards is a writer, a teaching professor at Northeastern University, and an advocate for people with chronic illnesses. Her books are *Life Disrupted* and *In the Kingdom of the Sick.*

Sarah Ellis is the cofounder and CEO of Amazing If, a company with an ambition to make careers better for everyone. She and her business partner Helen Tupper are coauthors of *You Coach You* and the *Sunday Times* number one business bestseller *The Squiggly Career.* Together, Sarah and Helen host the *Squiggly Careers* podcast. Their TEDx talk, "The Best Career Path Isn't Always a Straight Line," has more than 1 million views. Sarah has studied at Warwick Business School, London Business School, and Harvard Business School and has an MBA with distinction. Sarah is also the cochair of the Mayor of London Workspace advisory board.

Jenny Fernandez is an executive coach, chief marketing officer, and adjunct professor at Columbia Business School and New York University. Jenny's mission is to help successful leaders and their organizations drive exponential growth by unlocking resilience, collaboration, and innovative thinking. Jenny has more than 20 years of experience managing multimillion-dollar businesses and organizations at Mondelez International, Kraft Foods, Merlin Entertainments, and Loacker. Connect with her on LinkedIn.

Michelle Gibbings is bringing back the "happy to workplace" culture. The award-winning author of three books and a global keynote speaker, Michelle is on a mission to help leaders, teams, and organizations create successful workplaces where people thrive and where progress is accelerated.

Luciana Turchick Hakak is an assistant professor at the School of Business of the University of the Fraser Valley. Her research interests lie in the distinct but often complementary fields of diversity in the workplace, work-related identity, and stigmatized work, and she has specifically investigated these issues in the context of how immigrants fare in new work environments.

Lara Hodgson is the cofounder, president, and CEO of Now and the coauthor of *Level Up: Rise Above the Hidden Forces Holding Your Business Back.*

Mark Horoszowski is the cofounder and CEO of MovingWorlds, a social enterprise that helps corporations achieve their social, environmental, and governance targets by engaging, educating, and empowering their employees.

Rebecca Knight is currently a senior correspondent at *Insider*, covering careers and the workplace. Previously she was a freelance journalist and a lecturer at Wesleyan University. Her work has been published in the *New York Times*, *USA Today*, and the *Financial Times*.

Mita Mallick is the head of inclusion, equity, and impact at Carta. She is a LinkedIn Top Voice and a cohost of the *Brown Table Talk* podcast. Her writing has been published in *Adweek*, *Fast Company*, the *New York Post*, and *Business Insider*.

Art Markman is the Annabel Irion Worsham Centennial Professor of Psychology and Marketing and vice provost of continuing and professional education and New Education Ventures at the University of Texas at Austin. He has written over 150 scholarly papers on topics including reasoning, decision-making, and motivation. His most recent book is *Bring Your Brain to Work: Using Cognitive Science to Get a Job, Do It Well, and Advance Your Career* (Harvard Business Review Press, 2019).

Lesli Mones is an executive coach, a leadership consultant, and the founder of the P2 Leaderlab, an organization that helps women skillfully use their personal power for greater organizational impact.

Palena Neale is the founder of unabridged, a Paris-based leadership coaching and mentoring practice that helps professionals use their power and potential for greater personal and social impact. She researches and teaches on topics related to women's leadership. Her latest online course for women is Network to Amplify V.A.L.U.E. You can follow her on LinkedIn and Twitter @PalenaNeale.

Janice Omadeke is the CEO and founder of The Mentor Method, an enterprise platform helping companies keep and develop their diverse talent using the proven power of mentorship. She has also been featured in *Forbes, Entrepreneur* magazines, and she was a subject matter expert at the 2016 White House Summit on Building the Tech Workforce of Tomorrow.

Brenda Peyser has held leadership positions in the corporate world and academia for over 30 years. Most recently, she was a professor of communications at Carnegie Mellon, where she also served as associate dean of the School of Public Policy and Management and was the founding Executive Director of Carnegie Mellon University Australia.

Janet T. Phan is a senior technical product manager and the founder of Thriving Elements, a global nonprofit that connects underserved, underrepresented girls with STEM mentors. Janet's TEDx talk is titled "3 Key

Elements to a Thriving Mentorship." She's the author of *Boldly You: A Story About Discovering What You're Capable of When You Show Up for Yourself.*

Trish Ruebottom is an associate professor at the DeGroote School of Business at McMaster University. Her research interests lie at the intersection of social innovation and organization, specifically exploring the ways we organize to create social change. Her recent work examines the role of entrepreneurship in stigmatized industries.

Madeline Toubiana is an associate professor and the Desmarais Chair in Entrepreneurship at the Telfer School of Management at University of Ottawa. Her research program focuses on what stalls and supports social change. More specifically, she examines the role of emotions, entrepreneurship, institutional processes, and stigmatization in influencing the dynamics of social change.

Helen Tupper is the cofounder and CEO of Amazing If, a company with an ambition to make careers better for everyone. She and her business partner, Sarah Ellis, are the coauthors of *You Coach You* and the *Sunday Times* number one business bestseller *The Squiggly Career.* Together, Sarah and Helen host the *Squiggly Careers* podcast. Their TEDx talk, "The Best Career Path Isn't Always a Straight Line," has over 1 million views. Helen is also a trustee for Working Families charity and was previously awarded the Financial Times' 30% Club Women in Leadership MBA Scholarship.

Luis Velasquez is an executive coach who works with senior leaders and their teams to become more cohesive, effective, and resilient. He is the founder and managing partner of Velas Coaching, a leadership facilitator at the Stanford University Graduate School of Business, and a former University professor, and a research scientist. He is the author of the upcoming book *Ordinary Resilience: How Effective Leaders Adapt and Thrive*. Connect with him on LinkedIn.

Lise Vesterlund is a professor of economics at the University of Pittsburgh and director of the Pittsburgh Experimental Economics Laboratory. She founded and directs the Behavioral Economic Design Initiative. Published in leading economic journals, her research has been covered by NPR, the *New York Times*, the *Washington Post*, ABC, the *Economist*, the *Atlantic*, the *Guardian, Chicago Tribune*, and *Forbes*.

Laurie R. Weingart is a professor of organizational behavior at Carnegie Mellon University. She has served as CMU's interim provost and chief academic officer and as a senior associate dean and director of the Accelerate Leadership Center. Her award-winning research has been covered by the *New York Times, Wall Street Journal,* and *Business Insider*, and published in top management and psychology journals.

Avivah Wittenberg-Cox is CEO of 20-first, one of the world's leading gender and generational balance consulting firms, author of *Seven Steps to Leading a Gender-Balanced Business*, and a Harvard Advanced Leadership Initiative Fellow 2022.

Lisa Zigarmi is an organizational psychologist and leadership coach. She helps leaders relate more deeply, decide more efficiently, and think with more creativity. She is the founder of The Consciousness Project.

Rebecca Zucker is an executive coach and a founding Partner at Next Step Partners, a global leadership development firm. You can follow her on Twitter @rszucker.

Women *at* Work

Inspiring conversations, advancing together

ABOUT THE PODCAST

Women face gender discrimination throughout our careers. It doesn't have to derail our ambitions—but how do we prepare to deal with it? There's no workplace orientation session about narrowing the wage gap, standing up to interrupting male colleagues, or taking on many other issues we encounter at work. So HBR staffers Amy Bernstein and Amy Gallo are untangling some of the knottiest problems. They interview experts on gender, tell stories about their own experiences, and give lots of practical advice to help you succeed in spite of the obstacles.

Listen and subscribe:

Apple Podcasts, Google Podcasts, Spotify, RSS